The Rights of the Dying

The Rights of the Dying
a companion for life's final moments

David Kessler

HarperCollins*Publishers*

HarperCollins books may be purchased for educational, business, or sales promotional use. For information please write: Special Markets Department, HarperCollins Publishers, Inc., 10 East 53rd Street, New York, NY 10022.

FIRST EDITION

Designed by Ruth Lee

Library of Congress Cataloging-in-Publication Data

Kessler, David, 1959–
    The rights of the dying : a companion for life's final moments / David Kessler. — 1st ed.
      p. cm.
    ISBN 0-06-018753-0
    1. Death—Psychological aspects. 2. Terminally ill—Psychology.
3. Terminally ill—Family relationships. 4. Death—Psychological aspects—Case studies. 5. Terminally ill—Psychology—Case studies. 6. Terminally ill—Family relationships—Case studies. I. Title.
BF789.D4K47   1997
155.9'37—dc21   97-1947

97 98 99 00 01 ❖/HC 10 9 8 7 6 5 4 3 2 1

For my parents
Joseph and Sophie
who live in my heart

Contents

The Rights of the Dying

- *The right to be treated as a living human being.*
- *The right to maintain a sense of hopefulness, however changing its focus may be.*
- *The right to be cared for by those who can maintain a sense of hopefulness, however changing this may be.*
- *The right to express feelings and emotions about death in one's own way.*
- *The right to participate in all decisions concerning one's care.*
- *The right to be cared for by compassionate, sensitive, knowledgeable people who will attempt to understand one's needs.*
- *The right to expect continuing medical care, even though the goals may change from "cure" to "comfort" goals.*
- *The right to have all questions answered honestly and fully.*
- *The right to seek spirituality.*
- *The right to be free of physical pain.*
- *The right to express feelings and emotions about pain in one's own way.*
- *The right of children to participate in death.*
- *The right to understand the process of death.*
- *The right to die.*
- *The right to die in peace and dignity.*
- *The right not to die alone.*
- *The right to expect that the sanctity of the body will be respected after death.*

Author's Note

I wrote this book hoping to familiarize the reader with the physical and emotional aspects of dying. No book should be used to diagnose a condition or to serve as a treatment plan for the dying. For medical advice and individual problems, you should consult your physician.

The stories in this book present the challenges that numerous patients, their families, and their friends have faced, as well as the insights that they and I gained. Those who have shared their lives, deaths, and experiences with me are my teachers. We can all learn from them. We can also be inspired and touched by their love and courage, their hopes, weaknesses, anxieties, fears, dreams, and agonies. Those of us who take this journey find it a rich, meaningful experience that teaches us as much about life as it does about the rights of the dying.

The names and other identifying information of patients have been changed to preserve their privacy. Many characters are a composite of different individuals. If a real name is used, it is with permission of the individual or is publicly known information.

Introduction

Death is the final journey we take in life; however, for me it has been a central character and its prominence has grown as each year passes. For those of us who work with the dying, death is like an unwanted visitor one gets to know quite well. My journey has been made up of experiences dealing with death professionally, as well as within my own family.

Death is a broad traveler in our society. It is sometimes the result of violence, sometimes a kind act of nature, sometimes the end of a long disease. We watch it in our homes on TV, we pay to see it on movie screens, and we play with it in video games. Perhaps we hope that the more we view it, the less we will fear it. Although death is one of our most painful encounters when we experience it personally in our lives, we are morbidly curious about it. Many of us flirt with it throughout life, challenging it by climbing mountains, flying planes, and racing cars. But no matter how much we flirt with it at a distance, we all know that one day we will encounter it. Until then, we experience it as a spectator. As my work has brought me closer to this unwanted visitor,

I have found more peace in death, and I hope you will find peace in your journey.

When I began working with the dying in hospice settings in the early 1980s, I thought of a hospice as a physical location, a facility where the terminally ill were cared for. Through my work, I came to realize that hospice is a philosophy, a way of caring for loved ones. For some, hospice means a more natural death. For others, it means avoiding aggressive medical care when the end is near. Still others associate hospice with pain management. But the practice of hospice has never been clearly defined. The majority of people still die in hospitals where they are given few rights, where their needs and concerns are often unknowingly overlooked.

Sitting at countless deathbeds, I recognized that many family members, health care professionals, and even those who were facing death were unaware of the needs and rights of the dying. If they sensed these needs and rights, they had little idea how to express or exercise them. I began to feel that the final months and minutes leading to the end should be a powerful place in life, not a time of victimhood. Through the years I have tried to restore power to those who are dying and their loved ones by explaining, incorporating, and expanding the rights of the dying.

The difficult step was introducing the rights into practice. Society and the medical system have removed us from the process of death. At the turn of the century, death was a familiar and natural part of our lives, occurring at home with, at best, a doctor's visit. But by the 1940s and 1950s, death had found a new home: the hospital. There, doctors treated a number of patients at once, while intensive care units made the latest technology available to the dying. During the

1970s, death was removed from the community, from the home, and from us as individuals.

In the 1980s death was turned into a cold, impersonal experience. Most of us were robbed of the opportunity to be close to our loved ones in the final days. It was then that the hospice movement started to spread. Growing numbers of people were brought home to spend their last days surrounded by family and friends.

In 1984, I decided to form my own home health care company, Progressive Nursing Services, one of the first to be dedicated to the needs of terminally ill patients, mostly those with AIDS and cancer. We began with one patient and three nurses, growing over the next eight years as the home health care movement expanded. At the time, many hospital nurses were uncomfortable with AIDS and with the dying in general. There were, however, a smaller number who were committed to the idea of hospice. I wanted to bring the hospice-minded nurses together with those who needed it.

Home proved to be a truly healing place, as it was for our great-grandparents. At home, patients could receive treatments they needed surrounded by the things and people they loved. Home became a healing place for people to die, with memories, pets, and loved ones by their side. Unfortunately, many people were being discharged to their homes without any preparation for what lay before them. Our job was to prepare them, comfort them, and administer their health care.

Today the hospice idea has been furthered by health care reform. Many hospitals, doctors, and insurers realize that dying at home is not only more comfortable and personal, it is also economical.

By the time I sold my company to a national firm in 1992, we had over three hundred nurses and more than one hundred patients on service. I now spend part of my time lecturing on death and dying, as well as counseling the dying, their friends, and their family. I talk to the dying, but as my mentor Elisabeth Kübler-Ross has taught me, mostly I listen. My experience, first as a nurse in hospice, later managing a company that focused on hospice care, has left me with a deeper understanding of where, how, and why we die.

Death is an inescapable part of life. We can't prevent it, nor can we prevent the inevitable pain of separation it causes. However, we can make the experience of death better, both for the living and the dying. I have spent most of my adult life helping to make death a more natural, comforting experience.

Most of us would say that death is a natural part of life until we come to our own death or the death of someone we love. We see death as an unnatural separation because we haven't been raised to see death as a natural event.

Our great-grandparents cared for the ill and dying, prepared and buried the dead, and mourned for them, all in front of their children. We have little direct experience with death. If we desire a more meaningful personal experience we must go back and learn the basics. Unfortunately, we have few practical resources to turn to. The first important piece of work was Elisabeth Kübler-Ross's groundbreaking 1969 presentation of the five stages of dying: denial, anger, bargaining, depression, and acceptance. The rights of the dying presented in this book add to this foundation and provide a starting point for further exploration.

We must continue to examine the meaning of death because death is central to the meaning of life. If death is an enemy that triumphs over us when our lives end, if death is a horrible trick of nature that defeats us and our health, then our lives are meaningless. But if we understand that we are born, we flourish, and when our time comes we die, we will live our lives from a meaningful place and live our deaths in a meaningful way.

No one can really claim to understand death, unless they have actually died. We're only observers until our time comes. What I teach about death is what I have learned from it. While my medical training touched on the subject, I learned most of what I know about death from the hundreds of people I have had the privilege of caring for, and sharing with, in these most precious, final moments.

I cannot help anyone avoid the experience or erase the pain of separation, but I can share what I've learned about death. I can tell you how important it is to be with your loved ones, whether you are dying or are comforting one who may soon pass away. I can help you overcome your reluctance to discuss death and teach you how to talk with the dying. I can help you maintain your hope and show you how to fight for the rights of the dying. And I can help you face death with dignity and inner peace.

In this book, we'll examine the physical and emotional experience of death, and in our pain, find a way to say good-bye. My goal is to restore power to the dying and their loved ones. If someone you love is facing a life-challenging illness, this book will help you understand the needs and feelings— as well as the rights—of the person dying. If you are dying, this book will help you feel less alone by showing you the paths that others are exploring. Understanding the rights of the dying will help you communicate, help you be clearly heard and understood, and give you a foundation to operate from in this confusing and challenging time of life. I hope this book will help prepare you for your own death or the death of a loved one, and I hope it will comfort you in one of life's most profound moments.

I recently had the privilege of visiting Mother Teresa's Home for the Dying Destitutes in Calcutta. Mother Teresa told me that her most important work is with the dying, because she considers life so precious. A life is an achievement, she said, and dying, the end of that achievement. It is one of the most important times of our life. I told her that I was writing this book and asked her what she thought I should tell people. "Tell them not to be afraid of the dying," she said. "It is very simple. The dying need tender loving, nothing more."

David Kessler
Los Angeles, California

I

A LIVING HUMAN BEING

The right to be treated as a living human being.
The right to maintain a sense of hopefulness, however
changing its focus may be.
The right to be cared for by those who can maintain a
sense of hopefulness, however changing this may be.
The right to die in peace and dignity.

Every day, in thousands of hospital rooms across the
country, family members gather sadly beside the beds of
loved ones who are dying of cancer, of AIDS, of pneumonia,
or of a myriad of other illnesses. Husbands and wives, parents, sons and daughters, grandchildren, brothers, sisters, and
friends sit and stand uncomfortably, wondering what to say,
what to do, what to feel, and what to think.

Finally someone mentions the patient, his disease, or perhaps the funeral. Horrified, someone else immediately halts
the conversation, insisting in a whisper that everyone go out
into the hallway to discuss "that." Invariably, as they begin to
leave the room, a surprisingly strong voice comes from the
patient's bed: "I'm not dead yet! You can talk to me. You can
talk *about* me. Just don't talk without me!"

Words like these are heard day after day in hospitals,
homes, and hospices. They're shouted in anger or whispered

as a plea, spoken in plaintive, demanding, or matter-of-fact voices. "I'm not dead yet. I'm still alive."

The dying want to be treated—and they have the right to be treated—as living human beings until the moment they die. But often we "bury them alive" by thinking of them as their diseases, by acting as if they are incapable of making their own decisions, by negating their opinions, by overlooking their desires, by withholding information from them, and by omitting them from conversations. Without realizing we are doing so, we rob them of their dignity, we rob them of their hope, and we rob them of their very humanity.

One of my earliest memories of hospice was a discussion I had with the parents of a man who was suffering from leukemia. He was in his late twenties, not much older than I was at the time. The older couple shared how they were putting a conscious effort into taking their cues from him and not letting their opinions overpower him. His mother told me, in a softened voice, "We have protected him from the day he was born, from childhood diseases, from traffic, from ignorance and poverty. We helped him become his own man. Now we want to protect him from death, but we can't. We must let this be his life and his death." While we should never deny that the dying are dying, we should also never treat them as broken or no longer whole. Despite their illnesses, despite the fact that they are dying, they are still whole human beings. Life ends at death, we must always remind ourselves, not a moment before. To do any less than treat the dying as living human beings until death is to take from them their self-images, their stories, their hopes, and their dignity. We must continue to see them as they see themselves, to listen to their stories, to support their hope, and to treat them with dignity.

IMAGES OF LIFE

Ten years ago I stood by my father's bed in the intensive care unit of a Sacramento hospital. It was 3 A.M. I had just flown in from Los Angeles after being told that he would not make it through the night. I remember stepping out of the elevator onto the intensive care floor—it had that stillness that all hospitals have in the middle of the night. Dad was unconscious as I stepped up to his bed. I looked down at this now frail little man. It was strange to see him so quiet and still, dominated by the large and noisy heart monitor and other machines. He had always been so vital, so strong. I sat by his bed, trying to understand that this was going to be the last night of my father's life. I couldn't comprehend life without him. I sat there crying when, perhaps in response to my tears, he woke up and asked: "What's wrong, David?" He said it as if I were a little boy again and he was the father who could make all my problems disappear. For just a moment, it seemed as if he didn't have to die.

As we spoke about his situation, he told me that he was ready to die. My emotions were conflicted. I was terrified of losing him, yet glad that he was prepared to move on with peace of mind. He also told me something I had never thought about before. "Every morning," he explained, "when I wake up I feel like I'm twenty-seven again. Then I realize, of course, that I'm an eighty-four-year-old man. But I think of myself as being twenty-seven, not an old man with a bad heart. That's how I picture myself. And that's how I want to be treated. Not as the old man, the heart victim about to check out. No matter what's happening to my body, I still think of myself as a strong, whole human being. I want to be treated that way."

Nothing specific happened to my father at age twenty-seven. It wasn't the height of his career; he didn't win an award or invent anything. But it was a time when he was full of life and hope, a time when the future was waiting to be discovered and enjoyed. *I* looked at my father and saw a tired old man who was ready to die. *He* looked inside of himself and saw a twenty-seven-year-old youngster ready to live. That was the way he would always see himself. And that was how I had to see him, too.

We each carry an image of ourselves in our heads. It's "who we are" in our minds, a picture formed before we grew older, when we were most full of life. We see ourselves as something that transcends what we're going through. And we continue to see ourselves at our fullest times of life, no matter how old we may be or how ill we may have become. We cling to that part of ourselves that is indefinable and changeless, that does not get lost and does not deteriorate with age or disease.

An elderly woman with terminal cancer may see herself as a little girl on a swing with her feet reaching for the sky, as a beautiful young woman standing at the altar, as a proud mother helping her baby take its first step. We may see her as an old lady with an oxygen mask on her face and an IV needle in her arm, laboring to breathe and unable to walk. What we see when we look at her is disease and impending death and so we often refer to her as "my dying mother" when we ought to say "my mother, who is dying." Thinking of her as "my dying mother" limits her, in her mind and ours. She is and always will be a complete human being who happens to be dying. To think of her in any other way diminishes her, makes us see her as less than a whole person, casts doubt upon her mental competence, prematurely takes away the wonderful woman who *is still* our mother. The image is as important to us, her husband and children and siblings and friends, as it is to her.

We each have a self-image, which is where our story begins. We all have tales that explain who we are, what we think, what we dream of, what we fear, what family has meant to us, what we've accomplished, what is yet to be done, what we're proud of, what makes us laugh, and what makes us cry. Part of being a human is having those stories to tell. We tell them all the time, to family, to friends, and to strangers. Storytelling is a primal human need that does not diminish as our bodies weaken.

The stories we have are who we are and they are what survives our death. No matter what our religion or culture, our stories will be told when we die. The telling may be in the form of a eulogy, an obituary, or a monument. Whatever form it takes, the story will be told at least one last time.

We tend to forget that the dying still have stories to tell. Just as the healthy tell bits and pieces of their stories every day, people facing life-challenging illnesses want to tell us who they are, what they did for a living, about their families, their hopes, their dreams, their regrets. A very busy nurse who has little time to talk to her patients told me that she once finally stole a few minutes to speak to a frail old woman she was caring for in the hospital. The nurse was surprised and delighted to learn that forty years ago, her patient had won an Olympic gold medal for distance running. "I never saw her the same way again," the nurse told me. "There was so much more to her than I ever imagined."

We often don't listen to these stories because we think of the storyteller as being that eighty-four-year-old man with a bad heart; we think the story has ended. We look at the outer shell rather than the inner spirit—the twenty-seven-year-old man embracing life. Listening to the stories of the dying brings out their dignity and humanity. They have beautiful images of themselves, filled with stories to tell. We must continue looking and listening, until the end, for their sake and for ours.

Often we find ourselves distracted by a loved one's physical appearance. It is common to feel terribly uncomfortable at the sight of a loved one disfigured by illness or accident. The best thing to do under those circumstances is to look into the eyes of the loved one and see those changeless brown or green or blue eyes. Even when the body has deteriorated, you can usually see the person inside by looking into the changeless eyes.

Raj Neesh, a spiritual teacher, once said that the sky is always blue. Dark clouds come in and out. They may obscure our view but they are only temporary. When we look at the sick, we tend to focus on the dark clouds, forgetting that somewhere beyond is the ever-blue sky. The dark clouds of illness may come and go, the body may become disfigured, but the eyes are the window to the soul.

When our loved ones first become sick, it is easy to see them as being whole people with a little bit of disease. As the illness progresses, however, our loved one seems to become less of a person and more of the disease. We begin to have difficulty seeing the whole individual. At that point, when things are toughest, seeing our loved ones as whole means the most to them. Seeing beyond the illnesses is one of the most meaningful gifts we can give them. It is a greater gift to ourselves.

THE POWER OF HOPE

I recently took a tour of cancer clinics in Tijuana. About twenty of us boarded a bus in Pasadena, California, and headed toward the Mexican border, stopping to pick up more people in San Diego. As I spoke to my fellow passengers, most of whom were women, I learned that they were well-educated professionals with financial resources. Challenged by cancer, they were looking for alternative treatments that might save them.

Sally, an attorney in her early fifties, was hoping to find a cure for her uterine cancer. Despite a hysterectomy, the cancer had spread, and she was not expected to live. A thick file containing copies of her laboratory test results was stuffed into her purse.

Thirty-six-year-old John had melanoma, a cancer which began as a mole that changed colors. His doctor had looked at it and told him not to worry. Several months later another doctor noticed it, performed a biopsy, and discovered that it was malignant. The delay in treatment had given the cancer time to spread. When I asked him, "What brings you on this trip?" he answered simply, "Hope."

We saw eight clinics during our day in Tijuana, each one offering alternative treatments based on laetrile, shark cartilage, colonics, and diet. All of the clinics offered hope, the one thing that these people were not getting from their own doctors.

Our lives are based on hope. It is also the primary way in which we try to control death. We try to control the "when" of death with the hope for a cure. When we lose that, we hope to control how, where, and with whom we die. We hope that we won't lose control over our lives as we move into our last months or days. We hope that it won't hurt too much. We hope that our loved ones will be able to get along without us. We hope that we won't be alone at the end.

Hope and fear grip everyone who struggles with a life-challenging illness. The two emotions are as inevitable as they are constant, right up to the moment of death. If we take away someone's hope, we leave them with nothing but fear.

Greek mythology tells us that a maiden named Pandora was given a box by the gods but was forbidden to open her lovely gift. Unable to control her curiosity, Pandora lifted the lid, just a little. Out flew disease, plague, famine, floods, and all the other misfortunes and tragedies of the world. Horrified, she tried to slam the lid shut, but it was too late. Only one thing remained inside the box: hope. Pandora then released hope to the world. Hope is our gift from the gods. As long as we're alive, until the last moment, we can have hope. It's our right.

Unfortunately, we often diminish that hope by negating, by judging, or by denying. We rob the dying of their right to hope when we insist that they "face reality," or when we plead with them to "stop looking for miracles."

When Sally told her husband that she was going to investigate the clinics in Tijuana, he said, "Well, that's a big waste of time." He didn't realize that he was chipping away at her hope. He didn't understand that the outcome of the search is not nearly as important as the search itself. Hope is a journey, not a destination; its value lies in the exploration. Hope is the way we live life, and the journey of hope should last until we end.

This is very hard for loved ones and the medical community to understand. Our thinking is limited: we only see hope in a cure, and we feel hopeless when we believe there is none. The dying, however, see the value of living hopefully rather than hopelessly, and that is why they choose hope as their companion on the final journey. Many find hope in support groups, where a shared hopefulness improves the quality of life. Others find hope in faith and spirituality.

Even when the end is in sight, the dying have a right to hope. Regardless of whether or not we think that hope is valid, it is something we should protect. Hope should never go away, but what we hope for can change. First we may hope to recover; then we may hope for a peaceful death. We may hope that the children will be all right, and we may hope that there is a heaven.

Hope and reality needn't clash. You don't have to tell lies in order to keep hope alive. I've sat with hundreds of people who were in their last days, hours, or minutes, and I never once said, "There is no hope." Instead, I say, "It looks like you're going to die, but there's still the possibility of something happening. It's okay to hope." When given this permission, the terminally ill often explore their hope for healing or for a cure, then move on to talking about what kind of death they're hoping for should they not be cured.

Hope should always be cultivated and never challenged. We can live for weeks without food, days without water, but we can only live hours without hope. As long as it is nourished, hope is like a strong vine that can grow over and around obstacles. There are so many obstacles standing in the way of our loved ones' having hope that we needn't add more by being "realistic" or by playing "devil's advocate." Allow those who are challenged to find the paths that are best for them. Help them use their hope well.

Everyone has the right to hope for a miracle until he or she dies, and miracles do occur. When Patricia was lying in a hospital bed, her family knew it was time to say good-bye to her. She had acute leukemia, she was on a respirator, and she needed drugs to keep her blood pressure up and her heart beating regularly. Having seen death take hold many times, I could tell that she was going to die. But even though she was completely dependent upon machines and medicines, something inside of Patricia was not ready to leave. Nothing specific happened to turn the situation around, but she recovered and went into remission. She is now at home with her family. She still has cancer, but she's backed away from death's door. Miracles do occur. I know, because I have seen them.

DOCTORS AND HOPE

Just as the dying have a right to hope, they also have a right to be treated by physicians and nurses who can maintain a sense of hopefulness, however changing this may be. Finding doctors who are good at inspiring hope can be difficult, because medical professionals have been taught that death is the enemy, that they should "fight, fight, fight!" until the end. To many of them, death is the opposite of life, a terrible scourge to be destroyed, a failure—their failure. Once they decide that they can do no more for a patient, they tend to give up hope.

But hope is much more than an optimistic request, a guarantee of a cure or remission. Hope is a part of who we are, a part of our lives, and a vital part of our deaths.

Tall and silver-haired, seventy-year-old Sara was a retired college professor. She had a loving husband, Hugh, and three grown children. Although she no longer taught, she remained active in academic affairs. Shortly after her seventieth birthday, Sara learned that her abdominal pain and cramping was caused by a large tumor, surrounded by numerous smaller ones, in her abdominal cavity. The large one could be surgically removed, but it would be only a matter of time until one or more of the smaller ones became life-threatening.

Sara and her family accepted the fact, as best they could, that she was facing a terminal illness. A few days later, however, a friend told Sara about an experimental drug that might shrink tumors. Sara discussed this with her physician, who downplayed the possibilities. "Sara, face it," he said compassionately. "There is no more hope."

She paused, then seemed to inflate herself with strength that arose from somewhere deep down inside. "My hope is mine. I've had it all my life. Sometimes it becomes reality, sometimes it's just hope. I plan to keep my hope. In fact, I plan to die with it. So we can evaluate this experimental treatment, but not my hope."

Some otherwise good doctors destroy their patients' hope by telling them not to seek alternative treatments. Other doctors, unable to study and adopt every new idea that comes along, still remain open to new possibilities. When the AIDS epidemic began back in the early 1980s, many of the cancer and infectious disease specialists admitted that they had no answers and were willing to let their patients explore alternatives. If asked about other treatments, they said: "I don't know about the alternative therapies you're asking me about, and I cannot endorse them. But please let me know if you try them and I'll monitor your progress and your lab results. We can learn together." This approach helped to keep hope alive and helped many people to improve the quality of their lives.

Unfortunately, we haven't seen as much of this openness with other doctors. Many of the people on the trip to Tijuana were afraid to tell their doctors what they were doing. They felt their doctors would disapprove, and perhaps even refuse to continue caring for them. Instead of an "either-or" situation (do what your doctor recommends, or you're on your own), it would be nice to see an "in addition to" situation in which doctors feel comfortable allowing their patients to try alternative therapies and monitoring the results.

Some patients need an abundance of hope and numerous options. They may need to consult with the next doctor, try the next therapy, or travel across the border. Simply being told that one has a life-threatening illness ravages hope. A dying person has to grapple with the fact that he is, for example, not going to live a long life, that his retirement dreams will never come true, that he is not going to write that great novel or sail around the world, that he will never see his grandchildren, that he may not see his own children grow up—or that he may never even have children. These realizations tend to diminish hope. We must help the person who is dying hold on to the hope that is left.

Like Sara, we all have the right to live with our hope and die with it.

HOPE AND PURPOSE

Hope is intimately connected with purpose in life. If you ask people who are fighting to live why they want to continue living, you'll see that some have very strong purposes and goals, good reasons to remain alive. Others will examine their lives and realize that they have been getting up in the morning only because the alarm has been ringing. One person may immediately be able to tell you what her purpose is, another may have to think about it, while still another may not really know.

Some people will say, "I'm lying in bed. I'm not productive. I'm not helping my grandchildren. What purpose is there to my life? What lessons am I supposed to be learning?"

Purpose can be as much about who we are as about what we do. Our reason for being is not always tied to being productive or helping grandchildren. Remove one grain of sand from the beach, and the whole beach changes. Each person matters. Just by existing, we all change the world. Thinking about purpose helps people to realize that life itself is purposeful, and that there is a reason for everything. But the answer lies in the question, not the "answer."

I remember speaking with Jonathan, a college student who felt hopeless and worthless as he watched his older sister Mary being ravaged by cancer. "I don't understand," he protested. "Why is Mary lingering on in so much pain? What purpose is this serving? Why doesn't she just go already?"

It always seems cruel when someone lingers on, suffering or in pain. But we don't know what that person is here to learn, to teach, or to experience. Perhaps Mary lingered because she had taken care of Jonathan and his mother for years without asking for anything in return and was now supposed to do nothing but receive their love and care. Maybe Mary struggled to remain alive because she was afraid that her mother and brother would suffer too much when she died. Or maybe no one had told Mary that it was all right to die, that everyone would be okay if she were to move on. Hanging on to life for fear of hurting our loved ones is a powerful purpose; many have passed in peace soon after being told that their loved ones understand what is happening and that they will be all right.

I met an elderly woman in the last year of her life. I say we "met" despite the fact that she was in a coma during the entire eleven months I "knew" her. When she died, I remember thinking that there had been no purpose to this lengthy coma. Some years after she passed away I ran into her daughter, who shared with me how she, her two sisters, and her two brothers had led very individual lives, seeing one another only at the occasional Christmas or wedding celebration. "While I wish Mom had not been in that coma," she said, "we became a real family because of it. In that last year, we all pitched in to help and really supported each other. If it had not happened that way, we would have remained strangers who just happened to grow up together. I feel that there really was a purpose to that horrible year; it was Mom's last gift to us."

THE DIGNITY OF LIFE

As people's physical condition deteriorates, their rights should not. We tend to equate a loss of physical capability with a lack of mental and emotional capabilities, and then we treat the dying as less than the living. Being unable to speak anymore, for example, does not mean that you can no longer think. That's why doctors, nurses, and physical therapists are trained to talk to comatose patients as if they were fully functional human beings. They'll say, "Mrs. Smith, I'm turning you over now," or "Mrs. Smith, I'm massaging your back." It's important to remember that Mrs. Smith will remain a human being throughout this process. Although no longer fully functional, she is still a human being who deserves to be treated with dignity.

Being treated with dignity means being included in conversations about one's death and the decision-making process. We often try to protect the dying by excluding them from these conversations. We go out of the room to discuss what we're going to do with Mom, for example, feeling as if we're somehow protecting her by not allowing her to know about and participate in the discussions about her care. But we're not protecting her. Whatever happens as a result of that conversation, happens to *her*. We actually harm Mom by denying her the right to make her own decisions, by acting as if she were too fragile or incompetent to participate in her own life. We strip her of her dignity and her rights as a human being by leaving her out of this process.

Being treated with dignity means being treated as a part of the family. Many people are like Barry, a thirty-two-year-old television lighting designer who didn't want to tell his dying father that his marriage was on the rocks. "What's the point of telling Dad?" Barry demanded. "It will only upset him. He's old and sick. Why bother him with my troubles?"

When Barry finally told his father about his bad marriage, his father was very supportive and understanding. They had a great discussion that would never have occurred had Barry continued "protecting" his father. Once the topic was brought up, the father told the son about an experience that he'd had in a bad marriage that Barry never knew about. The two men enjoyed a loving interaction that was possible only because the father was allowed to continue being a part of the family. We forget that sharing and helping each other are what life is all about.

Life can have wonderful surprises if we don't put up walls because a loved one is dying. A mother never felt comfortable telling her children that, before she was married, she had put her first child up for adoption. At the end of life, touched by her children's care and kindness, feeling more dignity than ever, she let them know the truth. Today, the mother is gone, but her children have a newfound brother.

Being treated with dignity means being fully included in all aspects of life, regardless of the level at which one can participate. Anthony Perkins struggled with being treated as less than a whole human being. I remember having dinner with him one night in his rustic, hillside home. A few pieces of movie memorabilia hinting at his long, successful career were here and there, even a tiny "Bates Motel" sign half-hidden by the kitchenware. While cooking, he shared with me his fear that his disease would prevent him from working and supporting his family, from participating fully in life. He told me he was afraid that people would not hire him because he would be seen as ill. (At the time, he was quite healthy.) While the stigma of AIDS was a factor in Tony's case, most everyone with a deteriorating disease is seen as being capable of less, and is excluded from more and more of life. All I could do was listen, for I knew that what he was saying was true. Later that evening we were joined by his loving wife, Berry, and their two children, who saw him as being very much alive. They continued seeing him that way right up to the moment we watched life finally leave his body.

Michael Landon also fought against the notion that those with life-threatening illnesses are already dead. Shortly after the news of his inoperable cancer of the liver and pancreas was made public, Michael appeared on "The Tonight Show," full of humor and energy, joking about his condition and talking about his new television series. He told the world that my staff had given him a blood transfusion earlier that day, to keep his strength up. His openness and honesty gave America a different look at people challenged with cancer. He said "I'm not afraid to use the c-word, cancer," and he talked frankly about what was happening to him. He kidded about being treated with carrot juice and coffee enemas, and about the letter he received suggesting a "sexual cure." People could see that he was fully participating in life, pursuing his career, keeping in touch with his fans. He wanted to be seen as fully alive, and he was.

I never meet a "dying person." I meet Sara and Anthony and Sally. I meet elderly people dying of "old age," young people struggling with AIDS, and children afflicted with terminal cancer. I meet some people who want to fight to the end, and others who are content to pass quickly, with little struggle. I don't see them as being any different than your child, your uncle, or your boss. I see them as people. Despite their illnesses, despite the fact that they are dying, they are still whole people. Treating them as such preserves their dignity and their hope. Human beings deserve tenderness, dignity, honesty, compassion. And most of all, they deserve an acknowledgment that life ends at death and not a moment before.

I recently visited Elisabeth Kübler-Ross at her desert home. Suffering from a stroke and a fractured hip, she is confined to her home. A hospital bed dominates the family room. In her favorite chair, she sat and we spoke. Lighting her Dunhill cigarettes, she told me that she is now facing the same issues to which she has devoted her life, and which she has discussed in numerous books. Only this time, *she* is the one facing death. As we sat watching the sun set, she asked me to describe the book I was writing. I told her that it discusses the rights of the dying and asked if she had any comments or advice. "If we could remember to treat the living well," she replied, "we wouldn't need to remember the rights of the dying."

2

EXPRESSING EMOTIONS

*The right to express feelings and emotions about death
in one's own way.*

We tend to have trouble expressing our emotions and feelings in the best of situations. We have even more difficulty accepting the feelings and emotions of others. These feelings become even more difficult in times of crisis, when our fears are realized and our feelings are raw. We are afraid to express ourselves. We fear we'll be abandoned, and we fear that our feelings will be bottomless. But if we express ourselves during the dying process, what we share during these difficult moments will be our greatest comfort later.

We have a primal need to express feelings. As death approaches, the need to share and to speak from the heart grows. We rob both ourselves and those around us when we erect barriers to intimacy. It is not only the job of those who will live to comfort those who will not. Just as we comforted each other in life, we should continue doing the same as death approaches. Even though we don't know how to say good-bye and we don't want to say good-bye, if we can break through our reluctance and find the courage to express our emotions, we can bring our relationships to new levels. We can complete them. Sharing emotions while grieving together is not surrendering to death. Grieving in each other's arms can raise us to new heights of intimacy and love.

TALKING TO THE DYING

Our tremendous discomfort with death can make it difficult or impossible to talk with a dying person about what's happening. Many times, family and friends talk about everything *except* the fact that someone is dying. I often go into a hospital room, alone with the patient, and ask: "What's happening?" Many of them calmly reply: "I'm dying." Others are sarcastic or angry or frightened, upset that I seem to have missed the obvious. But in every case, the topic of death is opened. When I say, "Your family and friends think that you can't talk about dying," they usually reply, "No, *they* can't talk about it." And then we have discussions about disease and dying that later amaze their families. They wonder how their loved ones can talk about death with a total stranger, but not with them.

Being nervous about talking to a person facing a life-threatening illness is understandable. Most of us are afraid that what we say will be either too threatening or too trivial. I remember a mother who was losing her forty-two-year-old son, Steve, to leukemia just as he was becoming successful in his life and career. One day, in the hospital room, his mother mentioned that someone they knew had just purchased a wonderful new Mercedes. Steve looked up at her and said: "Do you have any idea how little a Mercedes matters to me now?" His voice was filled with anger that bewildered her. Was he angry at life for striking him down in his prime? Angry at his mother for being trivial? Angry at himself for not having had his own Mercedes? Angry because she had spanked him when he was a little boy? She never asked.

What do you say to the dying? Does talk about cars cheer them up or make them sad? Should you talk about things they used to do or used to want? About the latest laboratory results? The weather? You never know what someone needs when going into a conversation. The person you are talking to may not know either, for dying is always a new experience. The emotions of the person who is dying may change from day to day or moment to moment. If you do say, "I saw a great Mercedes," only to hear, "I don't care about fancy cars anymore," the more honest you can be, the better. It's fine to say: "I don't know what to say to you. Should we talk about baseball or your chemotherapy?"

It's all right to talk about dying if the person is receptive. Each situation has to be gauged individually. Not talking about death won't make it go away, but talking about it can bring life back into your relationship. Talking about death is like stepping into uncharted territory. It can be liberating and cathartic.

Even if you've never talked about anything deeper than the weather, you can speak from the heart. Howard and Bob were buddies who had lived next door to each other since they were children. They double-dated in high school and college and raised six children between them, both proud that they'd seen every home game of the Los Angeles Dodgers together since they'd retired. But they had never shared their feelings. When seventy-five-year-old Bob was dying of emphysema, Howard wanted to tell him how much he loved him. So Howard said: "You know, Bob, we played baseball as kids, we've been friends forever, our families grew up together, and we've shot the breeze for sixty-five years. Let me tell you, those have been great years. I really love you and I'm going to miss you."

Howard hoped those words would open the door to a genuine sharing of emotions. He said what he needed to say and gave Bob an opportunity to do the same. Howard's needs were independent of Bob's. Howard needed to complete the relationship, but Bob preferred to keep his feelings to himself to the very end. Simply hearing what Howard said was enough for Bob, and the two friends went back to watching the game on the hospital room TV, just as they had watched countless games before.

Sometimes there can be too much talk of emotions and pills and surgeries and death and dying. Sometimes it's best to say: "Hey, did you know that the Lakers won five in a row?" or "Did you see what Martha Stewart did on her last show!" There are no rules, except to play it by ear and listen to what the dying have to say.

LISTENING TO THE DYING

Allowing the dying to be heard is one of the greatest gifts that we can offer them. Medical professionals are taught that listening is a way of gathering information and assessing a patient's physical and psychological condition. Even more, listening itself is a powerful way of giving comfort. Loved ones and friends often arrive at the hospital in a panic, afraid to see someone who is facing death. Not knowing what to say, they often turn to the nurse or doctor and ask: "What do we do? What do we say?" The answer is always to listen, just listen. Listen to them complain. Listen to them cry. Listen to them laugh. Listen to them reminisce. Listen to them talk about the weather or talk about death. Just listen.

People who are facing life-challenging illnesses will tell you everything you need to know: how they feel about their situation and—if they're comfortable talking about it—how they would like to die.

Seventy-five-year-old Joseph suddenly began feeling weak. He called his son, Daniel, to say: "Daniel, I feel like something is wrong, more than just getting old. I don't want you to think I'm a foolish old man, but I think that my time has come. You know how we're always talking about going back to Maine, where I grew up and you were born? Let's go do that now. I'd like us to have some time together before I die."

"Dad, why don't you see your doctor?" the worried son suggested.

"I'll see him tomorrow," the father replied, "and then, can we go on the trip? Daniel, I'm seventy-five years old. I've had colds. I've had the flu. I've had arthritis. I know what old age feels like. This feels different. I can tell that something's seriously physically wrong with my body."

Daniel decided what to do. If he listened to his father and went on the trip, then found out that his father was all right, Daniel could live with the fact that they took a trip and everything was okay. But he felt that if he did not listen, and if something was wrong with his father, he would feel terrible about missing what might be the last opportunity for them to spend time together. He agreed to go on the nostalgic trip.

The next day, as promised, Joseph saw his doctor. Not sure what was causing the fatigue, the physician ran a number of tests. The results would be available in a few days. In the meantime, father and son drove up to Maine. They stayed in a motel not far from the lake where Joseph had grown up, and Daniel had spent his early years. They spent the week fishing, reminiscing, and visiting old friends. Despite his fatigue, Joseph talked a lot, and Daniel listened. Regardless of the outcome of the tests, after the first day on the trip Daniel was really glad that he was spending the time with his father. Neither dwelled on Joseph's fatigue. They simply had fun together.

A week later they sat together in the doctor's office, stunned to hear that Joseph had pancreatic cancer. At his stage of the disease, there was no cure or treatment that made any sense. In the next few weeks before his death, Joseph became progressively weaker, but both father and son took great comfort in the fact that they had taken the time to be with each other. Now, looking back, Daniel is grateful that he listened to his father, rather than responding in his usual way, which was to think that the old man was making a big deal out of nothing.

As we listen to those facing death, we hope that they will share with us their beliefs and thoughts, perhaps comforting us. But sometimes what they tell us doesn't comfort us. Sometimes we don't agree with what they tell us; sometimes we are disturbed to learn that their ideas on death challenge our own. Remember that the dying have the right to believe what they want and to express their feelings about impending death in their own way, even if their feelings are heartbreaking or devastating for us to hear. It is their right to live and die as they choose.

Thirty-six-year-old William Green found out that he was infected with the AIDS virus, HIV. He lived a number of years in good health, and likely had several years to go. An engineer, William researched the disease and the different options, learning that there were relatively few good treatments available at the time, the mid-1980s. He didn't tell his twenty-nine-year-old sister, Jennifer, about his disease until after a few years of good health. By then he had become more comfortable living with HIV. Once she knew, she was supportive and optimistic that medical science would save her brother.

One day William did not feel well. He went to his doctor, who diagnosed the flu. Within a week, however, the flu had not cleared up and William was looking worse. Alarmed, Jennifer urged William to call the doctor. But her brother said: "I know what lies ahead for me, whether it's today or tomorrow. I understand this disease. They can't do a lot for me right now, so there's no point in calling the doctor."

William's feelings about death disturbed Jennifer. She wanted him to fight until the last moment, but he didn't want to fight what he felt was a losing battle. He chose to let nature take its course, and he made it very clear that this was his choice to make.

A few weeks later William was having a great deal of difficulty breathing. Jennifer insisted on driving her brother, who was too weak to protest, to the doctor. The doctor, shocked to see how much William had deteriorated, started an IV, gave William oxygen, and arranged for him to be rushed to the emergency room. Jennifer demanded that her nearly comatose brother be placed on a respirator and that emergency measures be taken. Despite the best efforts of the doctors, William soon died.

Jennifer was in a "fight" mentality, but William was not. He had made his choice and expressed his feelings. Jennifer didn't like his choice and was unable to hear it, *but the choice was his.* By fighting his choice, Jennifer missed the opportunity to share her feelings with him about their lives together, to finish their business, and to grieve together.

We can cry with our loved ones, we can analyze treatment strategies, we can disagree, and we can deny the situation entirely, but in the end, the best thing we can do is to listen.

And when they tell us that the end is near, we need to listen even more carefully.

WHEN VERBAL COMMUNICATION IS NO LONGER POSSIBLE

Ultimately, we will cease to have the luxury of verbal communication. Due to illness, unconsciousness, or the nearness of death, our loved ones at some point will no longer be able to speak. Many assume that they no longer hear as well, simply because they don't seem to respond when spoken to. At this point, many people say that they wish they had said this or that, or had said "good-bye."

It is widely believed that hearing is one of the last senses to go, which is why medical professionals are taught to behave as if patients can hear right up to the end. When people ask me if their loved ones can still hear them, I always answer yes. If not physically, then they can hear you spiritually. They may not be alert, but if you say something from your heart, they will hear it in theirs.

You can still say what you wish you had said, even if your loved one is in a coma. Say it out loud if you can; if circumstances do not permit speaking out loud, say it in your mind. Much of our communication is nonverbal. Much can be said with a smile or a touch.

When you do talk to them, share your thoughts and feelings. Tell them things that would be of interest to them, such as the latest news or stories of mutual friends and family. Sometimes you may do a lot of talking, other times you may not. Don't be afraid of the silence. Holding hands or even just sitting nearby can communicate all that needs to be said.

WHEN SPEAKING IS TABOO

Saying what hasn't been said can bring us closer together. It also allows the dying to continue participating in life. He can still be a parent helping his children, a boy gently ribbing his brothers, a child impressing his grandparents. But these conversations don't always go smoothly. They can have unexpected repercussions, especially if they disrupt the family dynamics.

Since birth, Don suffered from a rare, degenerative liver disease. He had lived with it for all of his thirty-five years; it had never hampered his health or activities until an acute onset forced him to sell his real estate business and move back in with his parents. Although they gave their son total care, his mother and father never acknowledged that this was now a terminal situation.

Shortly after Don moved back into his parents' house, his younger brother, Mike, flew into town to be with him. The two brothers, who were close, had often spoken about the illness and its possible outcome. Don's condition deteriorated rapidly during his brother's visit. One day he and Mike were sitting in Don's bedroom when Don asked, "I'm getting better, aren't I?"

Mike looked him in the eye and sadly answered: "No, you're not."

"Well, how am I doing?"

Mike answered honestly: "You're dying." They discussed death and then, teary-eyed, they told each other that they were glad they were brothers. That's when their mother, Hannah, walked in. Without thinking, Don looked up at her and said: "I'm dying. Did you know that?"

Horrified, Hannah turned on Mike and snapped: "What are you doing to your only brother! Why are you coming in here and upsetting him like this?" In tears, she ran out of the room.

"Oops, now we've upset her," Don said.

Mike asked, "What happened?"

"Mike, you said the 'D-word.' Death is not supposed to be discussed."

"What should I have said when you asked me if you're getting better?" Mike asked. "Should I have lied?"

"Mom would have preferred that you said, 'Some days are better than others.' That's what they say."

Mike struggled with his conflicting emotions about what had just happened. He hadn't intended to upset the family. It certainly would have been inappropriate for him to have walked into a conversation between Don and their mother and said: "Today we're going to talk about death." But he had been speaking one-on-one with his brother, responding to Don with the same authenticity that they always had in their relationship all their lives.

Sometimes, in our effort to communicate, we will upset others—perhaps those that we love the most. Mike was in a difficult situation: there was no way to honor his relationship with Don without breaking the family taboo against admitting that the disease had become fatal. But when we feel it is time to talk about death, we should not hesitate to do so.

Although Mike and Don's mother was upset when the taboo was broken, I once walked into a hospital room to find a daughter thrilled that the subject had been opened by the hospital priest. "I didn't know how to bring it up with Mom," she said. "It's not something we ever talked about in our family. I'm glad the subject was open, so now we can talk about it."

Even though they may be difficult, the last days you spend

with your loved ones are ones you'll remember vividly. At times you may feel as if you're walking on eggshells, but everyone should be allowed to say what needs to be said. This is a sacred time because of the authenticity of the emotions that occur. We must let ourselves and our loved ones express feelings and emotions, no matter what the reactions may be. I am often in awe of the expressions of feelings between the dying and their loved ones. These feelings are among the purest found in life. Honoring these expressions is a holy obligation we have to each other.

MAKING RELATIONSHIPS CURRENT

At every stage of life, we find peace and fulfillment in our relationships that are current. A current relationship is one in which both have said everything they need to say to each other, whether it is supportive or challenging. Our relationships are current when we no longer harbor unexpressed feelings.

When there is a blockage in the relationship, however, when things have been left unsaid, we are bound to be uncomfortable and unhappy. That blockage and discomfort are most pronounced when things have been held back for years and someone is gravely ill. Ironically, most of us are less likely to make a relationship current when a person is ailing, for fear of doing harm. But if those unspoken thoughts are not expressed, they may never be. The urgency of illness is a golden opportunity to push through ancient blockages and talk openly and honestly.

Stan, a sixty-seven-year-old accountant, was struggling through painful and terminal prostate cancer. He was a charming storyteller, with an elfish grin and a twinkle in his eye that no amount of pain could erase. We often sat together in the living-room-turned-bedroom at his house, talking about this and that. As I got to know Stan and his wife, Joan, I could tell that she was struggling to suppress a huge undercurrent of anger.

I finally felt bold enough to say to Joan, "I sense you have a lot of anger." She admitted that she had never talked through some old but important issues with her husband, adding: "I can't discuss this with him now. He's so frail, he's so weak, he's lost so much weight. For me to go in there now and try to get even with him for the things I'm so upset about would be wrong."

I told Joan that there is a difference between getting it out and getting even. You can express negative feelings without hurting someone. When Joan realized that she had a right to express her feelings and that Stan had a right to hear them, she spoke with him. In a very loving way she told him why she had been suppressing anger for so many years. Not only did their discussion allow her to "get it out," it led to many other tender and loving talks.

Sitting by his bedside, she gently shared how she had felt judged by him during their many years of marriage. She felt that he didn't appreciate her, and that he was disappointed because she didn't have a career. He replied that it didn't matter to him whether or not she had a career, for he had always earned enough money. Then he pointed out the many successful ways she had used her talents. "You raised a family," he said. "You decorated our home, you decorated a design home for charity, you painted walls full of art for the children's hospital. Just because you weren't paid doesn't mean that you are not enormously talented, and that I don't appreciate you." The more they communicated, the more her anger dissipated. With the anger gone and the relationship current, there was more room than ever for love.

If a relationship is not current, we need to go back and say what we believe needs to be said. I saw how important this was while caring for Rose, a seventy-seven-year-old woman suffering from leukemia. Shriveled and shrunken down to only eighty-two pounds, Rose lay in a hospital bed we had brought to her home. She had suffered through two rounds of chemotherapy and other treatments, but was not doing well. Frank, her only child, was at her bedside that evening. He was startled when Rose, who had been too weak to talk or even move her head for days, suddenly lifted her head off the pillow and whispered urgently: "Frank! Frank!"

"Yes?" he answered, worried that she had been hit by a sudden pain.

"I never told you I loved you."

"But, Mom, I know you love me," he replied, puzzled.

"But I never *told* you," she said. With that she put her head back down on the pillow and closed her eyes. She didn't speak or move again, and she died the next day. Frank was perplexed. He didn't understand why it was so important for Rose to tell him that she loved him, when it was so obvious to him.

Rose *needed* to tell her son that she loved him. It was unfinished business she needed to complete in order to make their relationship current. Unfinished business consists of all those things we feel we haven't had a chance to say in our relationships. When serious illness arises, many people develop a need to finish the business of their relationships by communicating and sharing as openly as they can. When they don't, their survivors often spend the rest of their lives regretting that the business was left unfinished.

If you ask someone what needs to be said in order to make a relationship current, they usually don't have to think about it. They usually know what's been missing. They know that they're sorry for this or that, or that they haven't said thank you for being a caring parent or spouse or child or friend. They've never said, "I'm proud of you" or "You hurt me" or "We had difficult times, but I'm glad you are my friend." Now is the time to say it.

Making a relationship current can lead to life-changing breakthroughs. Other times, we just need to say something. What we say is not as important as giving ourselves permission to say it.

Elisabeth Kübler-Ross tells the story of a wife who reminisces about her husband. The wife remembers the time she dropped a blueberry pie on the carpet of his beloved car. She thought he would kill her, but he didn't. The wife remembers the time she dragged him to a dance he didn't want to go to and forgot to tell him to dress formally. She thought he would be furious, but he wasn't. She remembers the time she danced with his friend in order to make him jealous. She thought he would leave her, but he didn't. She wanted to tell him all these things when he returned from Vietnam, but he didn't return. Because she was unable to give herself permission to acknowledge these moments she felt that their business was never finished.

Sometimes, however, nothing needs to be said. If the relationship is current, just being there is enough.

GRIEVING TOGETHER

Cynthia developed terminal cancer of the cervix. As the end approached we had many open discussions about death.

During her last weeks, her old friend Anne would spend most of the days with her, then go out in the evenings with friends.

Cynthia and Anne were both open with their emotions. "I can't count the number of times we cried together," Anne said. "Or she cried as I listened, and I cried as she listened. I remember, toward the very end, my friends saying: 'It's odd about you and Cynthia. You don't seem very sad about her. You don't cry about her at all.'"

Anne immediately wondered what was wrong with her. "Cynthia was about to die. Why wasn't I crying with my friends? Then I realized that I had already cried all the tears that I had to cry in that moment with Cynthia, so I didn't need to cry later in the day. My grief was current, and so was our relationship. I always felt close and in the moment with Cynthia, and we had no unfinished business. In the evenings, when I went out with my friends, I wasn't shell-shocked and devastated. I was also in the moment with them, enjoying their company."

Many people don't want to burden ailing friends or relatives with their grief. Trying to remain strong, they become selfless, putting their emotions aside. But when these people tell me how sad they are, I ask: "Have you cried in front of him? Have you told him how much you're going to miss him, how sad you are, how angry you are?" They usually say no.

There is no reason why the relationship should not remain two-way until the end. Andrew lost his older brother Kevin several years ago. Although they had grown up together, one of Andrew's most cherished memories occurred a week before his brother died.

"He was only thirty-two when he was diagnosed with lymphoma. Through the many years of his illness, I felt it was my duty to become stronger as he weakened. I didn't think that I should allow my pain and sadness to show. That seemed selfish; after all, he was going to die, not me. My resolve to be 'brave' was strengthened as I saw him pouring all his energy into accepting and handling his own situation. I believed that adding my grief to his otherwise full plate would have been wrong. I tried so hard to be strong, not to cry in front of him. I was able to keep up the facade until a week before he died. Then I finally broke down. To my surprise, he comforted me and wiped away my tears. No words were spoken. The physical act of his holding me as I cried said it all."

It is a deeply moving experience to be comforted by the dying, one that can be extremely important to them. I remember saying to my father, shortly before he died: "I can't imagine a world without you." He said to me, reassuringly: "Don't worry, time will heal all." Being able to comfort me made him feel like a father again. Over the years since his death, often in my sadness, I can still hear his reassuring words.

We tend to look for comfort outside the sickroom and away from our loved ones. But we shouldn't deprive them of chances to be loving people. That's what they wanted to be in life, and that's what they continue to want to be until the end. By opening up we include them in our life and our grief. We are honest with them, and we honor them with our honesty.

We will grieve alone for the rest of our lives, missing them long after they have gone. There is a brief period, while they are dying, that we can grieve with them. Shortly after they have died, there is a period during which we can grieve with others. During my mother's final hospitalization for kidney disease, my father and I got to know a woman named Edith, whose husband was also in the intensive care unit. Soon after my mother died, Edith took me aside and said: "You've got to be strong for your father. Be very strong. Be a man, don't cry."

And so I was strong for my father. Though I was only twelve years old, I never cried in front of him. But I cried privately in my room, without my father knowing. And I heard him crying privately in his room, not wanting me to know that he was hurting. We *never* cried together.

Family members encourage each other to keep stiff upper lips, not to openly cry or grieve. I always suggest the opposite: Share your grief. Cry in front of someone, and cry with them. Witnessing grief gives the witness permission to grieve. When Peter lost his only son, the fifty-seven-year-old man sat stoically through the memorial service. It wasn't until a business acquaintance gave him a hug and, to Peter's surprise, began crying, that Peter also began crying. He knew that his colleague, also being a father, understood what a great loss this was. The two men sobbed together. In this moment, their closeness and understanding allowed their tears.

It's not a matter of *if* you will grieve, but *when* you will grieve. Don't miss the opportunity to grieve with another who shares your pain. Those who grieve well, live well.

WALKING TO THE GATE

In days not too long past, if a family member was going away we took them to the airport or train station, waiting with them at their gate until they left. The same was true when they arrived—we met them at the gate, not curbside or in the baggage claim area.

Today, we no longer walk people to the gate. We travel

more, and there are taxi cabs, airport shuttles, long-term parking, and lengthy security procedures. In the past year, I've tried to go back to old habits, taking my family to the airport and greeting them there when they return. When you've been out of town, away from your home and family, it's great to have someone you love meet you at the gate. Going to the airport becomes an act of love.

The concept of "walking to the gate" has much to offer with respect to life and death. Today's newborn is "met at the gate" by his father in the delivery room. The father hands him to the mother and may then cut the umbilical cord. Dad is no longer confined to or content to sit in the waiting room. Just as greeting the newborn at the "gate" is beneficial, we should do the same for the dying.

When Robert, a close business associate, found a suspicious lump near his spine, he was optimistic at first. We talked about the options for treatment, assuming it was a benign growth. Then Robert looked at me, really looked at me, and said: "What if it is the worst-case scenario? What if I am going to die?"

I searched inside for my most honest yet compassionate response. "Then, Robert, my friend, I will be there with you for as long as I can. I will walk you to the gate." Robert's time has not yet come, but he knows that when it does, he will not be alone.

Ninety-two-year-old June was living in a retirement home, just down the street from her son and daughter-in-law. The two "children," both in their late fifties, were always close to June. They visited her a number of times each week and took her out as much as possible on weekends. In fact, the daughter-in-law, who lost her mother when she was young, loved June for forty years like her own mother.

One day the retirement home's doctor examined June and ran some tests. He found that a tumor had wrapped itself around her aorta, the largest blood vessel in the body. Given her age and poor general health, none of the standard treatment options made sense.

Her son and daughter-in-law talked about this new development, then told June: "As you get sicker, we don't want you to go into a hospital and be cared for by people who don't know you. We want you to die in our home, with us around you. Between us and the kids, we'll manage. You've always been there for us, now we'll be there for you."

The idea of walking loved ones to the gate is gradually catching on. We walk our loved ones to the gate when we bring them home to die, rather than turning them over to strangers. We walk our loved one to the gate when we spend the night in the hospital room rather than waiting in the waiting room for them to die. We walk them to the gate when we let them know that no matter what happens, we will be with them. We finish our unfinished business when we say what needs to be said, we cry with them and for them, and we hold their hands as we walk them to the gate.

3

PARTICIPATING
IN DECISIONS

*The right to participate in all decisions concerning one's
care.*

*The right to expect continuing medical care, even
though the goals may change from "cure" to "comfort" goals.*

*The right to have all questions answered honestly and
fully.*

We're not used to thinking much about life, which is
perhaps why we give so little thought to dying. We die
whether we think about death or ignore it completely. But if
we choose to, we can have a say in how we die, where we die,
and what happens before and after. In so choosing we take on
the responsibility of participating fully in our care and in our
deaths.

The idea of planning your dying and death seems odd at
first. Yet we spend days, weeks, and months deciding where
to go to college, which house to buy, and whether to get married. Death is an equally important event. It's your choice
and your right to participate in all decisions concerning your
care and, if need be, the how and where of your death, but

you cannot die on your own terms unless you participate in your death. Participating in these decisions requires advance planning and tremendous determination.

MAKING DECISIONS

Ask yourself what your goals are as you enter into the final phase of life. Do you want:

- *to continue on exactly as before, with no thought of what will come?*
- *to pursue aggressive care and treatment?*
- *to allow nature to take its course, without requesting heroic measures or life-extending technologies?*
- *to take complete charge of your care?*
- *to let someone else decide what's best for you?*

The decision is yours to make, and whatever you decide is correct for you. You have the right to make any and all decisions concerning the way you die. No one can take the right to make those decisions away from you, but first you must claim that right.

Sometimes people make "dual" decisions, pursuing two goals at once, hoping that the first will come to fruition but prepared to accept the second if the first fails. Eighty-year-old Marty made such a decision when he discovered that a cancerous mass had invaded his lungs. An energetic oldster who played tennis, walked briskly every morning, and fished on the weekends, he began having small pains in his chest and back. At first he ignored the problem, chalking it up to old age. But the pain grew worse, and within one month of the first twinge he found himself at a major medical center, listening as the doctor clinically described the three-inch mass that was growing in his lungs. It had also spread to his liver, and was threatening to kill him.

His family was in shock. Lynn, his daughter, sobbed as she said that they had always thought "Dad would die of old age, not this." Marty and his family held a meeting to discuss a medical power of attorney and resuscitation. They agreed that if something drastic happened to Marty there should be no heroics and that he should be allowed to pass peacefully. It was a difficult decision for them to come to together. When they told me what they had decided, I asked if they had given these instructions to the medical staff. Like many others, they hadn't. We often make this decision among ourselves and forget to inform the very people who will have to act in the middle of the night when the heart monitor suddenly shouts out the alarm. Lynn verbally informed the staff of her father's and family's wishes.

When I came to visit the next day, I found Lynn and a nurse standing outside the door to Marty's room. The nurse, a friend of Lynn's, was scolding her. "Telling them not to resuscitate was a big mistake," the nurse insisted. "You should have let them finish the testing and present treatment options before you made a decision. Now they think your dad wants to die. They won't give him a complete workup."

I pointed out to the nurse that the family hadn't canceled any tests or made a final decision yet. "They've made a two-part decision," I said. "He doesn't want heroic treatment, but he doesn't want to be ignored either. If his heart gives out in the middle of the night, don't revive him. But otherwise continue with the tests, present the treatment options, and they'll decide from there."

The decision Marty and his family made was not in conflict with itself. It simply stated that the evaluation should continue *unless* he took a sudden, drastic, and irreversible turn for the worse. Some medical workers find this hard to understand, but it *is* possible to simultaneously fight the disease and bow to the inevitable, and it is your right to do so.

If you find yourself in the same situation as Marty and his family, tell the nurse or doctor in charge, "I would very much like you to continue treating my father, but if he suddenly takes a turn for the worse, I would not like him to be placed on a respirator." Emphasize that you want all the treatments possible *up to a certain point,* a point that you, the patient, and the doctor(s) agree on.

When you inform the staff of this or any other decision, always ask the nurse taking care of you or your loved one to note it in the chart. If the nurse is unavailable, ask for the charge nurse. Tell them that you want to inform them and all physicians of a decision you've made concerning care and that you would like it noted in the chart.

TAKING CHARGE

In a memorable scene from the movie *Terms of Endearment,* Shirley MacLaine plays a mother whose daughter is dying of cancer. "How is she?" she asks the doctor.

"I always tell people to hope for the best and prepare for the worst," the doctor replies.

Angry at this reply, Shirley snaps, "And they let you get away with that?"

Many of us let our doctors get away with telling us too little or limiting themselves to platitudes that are neither comforting nor informative. You can set goals and make decisions only if you know what's happening. *You have the right to have all questions answered honestly and fully.* Keep these actions in mind:

- 🦋 *Ask questions—and demand answers if they're not forthcoming.*
- 🦋 *Insist that your doctor sit down with you and your family to explain the situation and answer all your questions.*
- 🦋 *Get ready for the meeting by asking the nurse about your disease, reading about it, getting information off the Internet.*
- 🦋 *Come prepared with a list of questions.*
- 🦋 *Don't expect to be popular with the doctors you question.*

Open, honest, assertive, and questioning individuals who want information are not always welcome visitors in the medical system. Some doctors would prefer that you simply sign the consent forms and let them do what they feel should be done. One doctor routinely refuses to give test results to his patients. "Don't worry," he says when they ask. "I'll take care of you." Another, when a patient demanded to see the tests results, threw the chart on the floor and shouted, "I will not be questioned!" Should this or something similar happen to you, do the following:

- 🦋 *First, make an appointment to see the doctor in his or her office (or in your hospital room, if you are hospitalized).*
- 🦋 *At the appointment, explain that it is important to you to be informed and involved in your care and allowed to ask questions.*
- 🦋 *After the doctor reacts, ask if he or she is comfortable answering questions. If not, say that you may want to find another doctor, one more open to your participation.*

Fortunately, physicians' attitudes toward patients are changing. More and more, they expect and even welcome questions.

Many patients, however, do not ask. They can't imagine questioning physicians or telling them what to do. They don't realize how empowering it can be to stand up for what you believe in. This was the case with Rose, the seventy-seven-year-old woman who said, "I never told you I loved you" to her son. When Frank first brought his mother to the hospital, she had a fever and recurrent flulike symptoms. The day after she was admitted to the hospital, he received a message from the doctor. Unable to speak to the doctor by telephone, he immediately rushed to the hospital to make sure that his mother was all right. Two hours later the doctor arrived on his rounds. After cheerfully greeting the mother and son, he asked Frank to step into the corridor with him. There, the doctor explained that Rose had leukemia.

"But I was with her for two hours, and she never said a thing about it," Frank sputtered, frightened and puzzled.

"Well," the doctor replied, "I figured she's seventy-seven, what's the point of telling her now?"

Frank was furious. "The point! The point!" he shouted. "How about the point that this is *her* life."

"I'm just trying to protect her," the doctor replied huffily.

"She's lived seventy-seven years without your protection. She is very capable. She has the right to be involved in her life, her illness, and even her death, if it comes to that. Now, please, go in her room and talk to her!"

Sheepishly, the doctor went in the room to tell Rose that she had leukemia.

Sometimes the doctor is willing to be open with the patient, but the family takes him or her aside and says, "Let's not say anything." Physicians often agree to join the conspiracy of silence, rationalizing that they are sparing the patient agony. Everyone means well, but withholding knowledge from those faced with life-threatening illnesses keeps them from participating in all decisions concerning their care and excludes them from the final chapters of their own lives.

It is best when doctors sit down with their patients and say: "I wish I had different news, but I have to tell you that it looks like you are dying. I don't know when you are going to die. This is what I can do for you, and this is what I can't do for you. What would you like to know? How would you like to proceed?"

Information is a kind of medicine to patients who must make decisions. How can we expect them to decide whether to pursue aggressive or passive therapy if they don't know what lies ahead? How can someone with Lou Gehrig's disease (amyotrophic lateral sclerosis), for example, make a decision without knowing that the disease will eventually weaken the chest muscles so much that it will be uncomfortable to breathe?

Illness and death are never easy. Information may not change the course of your disease, but it will certainly help you chart your course through the difficult times ahead. That is why patients *must* be kept informed. And that is why patients must be willing to stand up to doctors who are unwilling to inform them. The stand may take the form of a simple, polite request. It may require cajoling, arguing, or shouting. Whatever it takes, insist upon knowing.

CHANGING GOALS

Whether or not you've decided to participate in your care, and whether or not you've learned all you can, *you have the right to expect continuing medical care, even if your goals change* from month to month, week to week, or day to day. You may make one decision when you first get the diagnosis and quite a different one after six months of chemotherapy. You may begin by insisting on "cure" goals and later realize that a cure is not possible and choose to adopt "comfort" goals. Perhaps you'll move in the other direction, changing your "do not resuscitate" (DNR) order to "do everything possible to keep me alive." *Your latest decision is the only one that counts.* You have the right to change your mind, and your changes of mind should be honored.

Unfortunately, our sluggish medical system does not respond well to change, and some people are forced to take unusual action. Tom, a forty-two-year-old man suffering from end-stage kidney disease, made no bones about the fact that he was manipulating his doctors when I spoke to him in his home. Having just taken over his care, I went to introduce myself and learn of his desires. What he told me was not unusual, although his bluntness was. "I'm having trouble making a final decision," he said. "I get scared of dying and go for a few weeks feeling like fighting to the end, then for a while I'll be tired of suffering and feel like letting nature take its course. But I can't find a doctor flexible enough to swing back and forth with me. They don't realize how frightening it can be to face death, they just get frustrated with me. So I have two doctors. When I'm feeling aggressive, like I want to keep going, I call 'Dr. Aggressive.' And when I just want my pain controlled while I let nature take its course, I call 'Dr. Mellow.' One doesn't know about the other, and I'm not going to tell them."

It would certainly be better to be looked after by one physician, but finding one who feels comfortable with your shifting goals can be difficult. I don't recommend Tom's solution, although I understand why he felt it was necessary. Instead, I suggest you find one physician who agrees with your treatment philosophy, who can accept your approach, and who can be flexible.

RESPECTING WISHES

Everyone has read in the newspapers of families going to court to force the doctors to remove the respirator from their loved one who has been lying in a coma for years. These legal battles can rage for months, ripping families apart, possibly forcing patients to remain "alive" against their wishes. The key issue is always the patient's wishes. Most people never make their wishes known. Mrs. Smith may think that her husband, who is now in a coma, wanted to go quickly and quietly, while her son believes that his father wanted to die fighting. When we can't ask Mr. Smith what he wants, we have to turn to lawyers and judges who have never met Mr. Smith and can't possibly know what he wants done.

Most people simply don't want to talk about death and dying. Talking about it means facing the fact that we or someone we love will die someday, perhaps soon. Sometimes we are even afraid that talking about it may make it happen. Many remain silent until they can no longer speak. Then someone else must make a choice and decide whether to keep the respirator and the other machines on or to switch them off. The choice usually falls to women, for they tend to out-live their husbands. Many women struggle to hold firm to their opinions in the face of strong-willed male physicians who have different ideas. Your wishes may not be respected if you make them known only to your spouse.

Patricia had recently come home after six weeks of hovering near death from acute leukemia in the intensive care unit. Since she had not made her intentions known and her body had been absolutely unable to do anything for itself, she was completely dependent on machines during that time. Yet somehow she recovered. Afterward, at her fiftieth birthday party, she looked radiant; she had a glow about her I had never seen before. After we hugged and kissed, she told me that she didn't remember anything that had happened to her in the intensive care unit, where she was expected to die at any moment. "My first memory is being back on the regular medical floor. I guess I just wasn't ready to go," she said with a smile. "I needed more time with my children. They're still so young, nineteen, seventeen, and fourteen. That sounds old, but it's not." I felt my eyes filling with tears as she continued. "I am so happy to see everyone and be here."

As I left the party I wondered if Patricia would issue clear medical directives now. She was so optimistic, so happy to be alive, she might have thought it was "wrong" to simultaneously prepare for life and death.

A month later she got the bad news: The cancer was back. Patricia chose not to address her situation, even when her family brought up the topic. It wasn't in her optimistic nature to give directives to stop the medical care. Instead, she made plans to face the cancer head-on.

Three days later Patricia went to sleep, but the next morning she could not be roused. Her husband, Peter, called the doctor on call, who told them to call 911 or bring her to the emergency room. The family sat vigil by her bedside at home all through the day, not knowing what to do. The next night she began her descent into death's arms. Panicked, they called 911, and the paramedics arrived just as she died. Seeing that she was clearly in end-stage cancer, they asked Peter if they should revive her. He looked down at his wife's cancer-worn body, then at his wife's brother for guidance. Her brother shook his head no, and the decision was made. It was a merciful, loving decision.

Patricia's family will never know if their decision was the right thing to do. They'll never know if it's what she would have wanted. That's why it's important to speak to your family, friends, and doctors about your wishes, to let others know exactly what you want to happen when you are no longer able to make that choice for yourself.

Emergency room physician Dr. Mark Katz deals with patients who haven't had time to express their wishes. He told me about a patient he treated one hectic day. Seriously ill, dazed, and unable to communicate, the man tried to push Mark's hand away as he struggled to insert a breathing tube into the patient's throat. He couldn't tell if the patient was trying to indicate that he didn't want any more care or if he was trying to swat away the uncomfortable instrument being stuck into his mouth because he didn't realize what was happening. Was it simply an unconscious reflex? "There was no way to know," Dr. Katz said sadly. "At the tail end of his life the man was unable to make his wishes known, and unable to choose the how, when, and where of his death."

We *can* make our wishes known, but so many of us are reluctant to do so simply because we don't want to address the issue. Others are afraid if they make their wishes known they will receive inferior care, or no care at all. This is very common among people traditionally underserved by the medical system. But if today we don't face the fact that we will die someday, we may find ourselves powerless to change what is happening to us tomorrow.

ADVANCED DIRECTIVES

If you find it difficult to talk about your wishes, you can express them on paper via documents known as an Advanced Directives or Durable Power of Attorney for Health Care. These documents speak for you when you cannot. They allow you to specify the level of treatment you wish to receive, anything from full heroic measures to nothing but painkillers to keep you comfortable as you pass on. You can also designate a proxy, a person who will make decisions for you when you cannot. This sample Advanced Directives put out by the California Medical Association offers three options from which you can choose:

I do not want efforts made to prolong my life and I do not want life-sustaining treatment to be provided or continued: (1) If I am in an irreversible coma or persistent vegetative state: or (2) If I am terminally ill and the application of life-sustaining procedures would serve only to artificially delay the moment of my death: or (3) Under any other circumstances where the burdens of the treatment outweigh the expected benefits. I want my agent to consider the relief of suffering and the quality as well as the extent of the possible extension of my life in making decisions concerning life-sustaining treatment.

or

I want efforts made to prolong my life and I want life-sustaining treatment to be provided unless I am in a coma or persistent vegetative state which my doctor reasonably believes to be irreversible. Once my doctor has concluded that I will remain unconscious for the rest of my life, I do not want life-sustaining treatment to be provided or continued.

or

I want efforts made to prolong my life and I want life-sustaining treatment to be provided even if I am in an irreversible coma or persistent vegetative state.

Unfortunately, having an Advanced Directive may not be binding if your family does not agree with your wishes. This was the case in the story of two brothers, Benjamin and Saul. A diabetic, sixty-seven-year-old Saul had been on kidney dialysis for several years. He had already suffered two heart attacks. His vision was rapidly dimming and he was in danger of losing his right foot to gangrene. The once robust man, a self-made millionaire several times over, barely had enough energy to walk from his bed to the bathroom.

One night Saul called his younger brother, Benjamin, asking him to come over right away. Benjamin did so, to find Saul lying in bed. Saul's wife, Phyllis, was not home. He looked very weak. His breathing was shallow and his heart beat weakly. The frightened younger brother said, "I'll get help," but Saul instantly replied, "No."

"Do you want to die?"

Saul nodded, adding, "Don't let them revive me." He pointed to a document on the nightstand. "There's my wishes in writing. It says not to revive."

Benjamin knew exactly what Saul was talking about, for they had spoken about this before. Saul was ready to die, but his wife, Phyllis, was not ready to let him go. Both men knew that she would ignore the "no resuscitation" Advanced Directive he had prepared. Saul wanted his brother Benjamin to make sure that his wishes were followed.

The younger brother sat by the older brother's bed, holding his hand and recounting their favorite childhood memories as he blinked back his tears. He knew that Saul had suffered greatly and was ready to go, but he didn't want to lose his brother. And he hated to be the one to ensure that he would, indeed, die. But he was prepared to do so.

Things went smoothly until Phyllis came home unexpectedly. When she saw what was happening she immediately called 911 for help. In no time at all the paramedics were there, demanding that Benjamin step aside and let them work on Saul. When Benjamin refused, they called the police.

"I'm his brother," Benjamin told the police officers. "I'm telling you that he wants to go. You can't touch him if he wants to go!" He held up the Advanced Directive. "Here are his wishes in writing!"

"Well, I'm his wife," Phyllis shouted, snatching away the document and ripping it to shreds. "And I say he wants to live!"

Benjamin turned to Saul, whose eyes were shut, and said: "Saul. If you want them to leave you alone, squeeze my hand." Everyone froze, silently, watching Saul's hand. It squeezed Benjamin's.

And so they continued doing battle, Benjamin and Saul against the rest. As long as Saul was conscious enough to squeeze Benjamin's hand, the paramedics had to stand back. But as soon as Saul was unconscious, Phyllis, the wife, would have control over the situation. Then the police could shove Benjamin aside and let the paramedics get to work. And so Saul fought to stay conscious as he died, hoping to remain cogent long enough to get close enough to death to make the paramedics' efforts useless. Every sixty seconds he squeezed

Benjamin's hand upon request, signaling that he wanted to die. And then he no longer squeezed.

"There!" Phyllis shouted. The policemen literally shoved Benjamin aside as the paramedics shoved needles and tubes into Saul's body, pumped him full of fluids, and shocked his heart. But it was too late. Saul had fought unconsciousness almost up to the end, ensuring that he would be allowed to die. The police threatened to arrest Benjamin but didn't.

Phyllis never spoke to him again, for she blamed him for her husband's death.

Brenda and her husband, Percy, had a much more pleasant parting. Brenda always believed in taking care of things ahead of time. When her breast cancer recurred, she handed Percy an envelope containing her Advanced Directives. He read her wishes, then they talked about them, planning what do in various situations. Shortly before she died, Brenda said: "I'm really glad that I had prepared those. It helped us talk about everything and agree beforehand. Then Percy and I could really enjoy the time we had left together with our children, without worrying about 'what ifs.'"

It's important to select a strong representative to safeguard your wishes, someone who will stand up for you, under pressure, even if they disagree with your decision. Your first instinct may be to assign that responsibility to the person closest to you, but that person is not always strong or decisive enough to carry out your requests. It's also vital that you discuss your wishes with this person *before* designating him or her as your proxy. Express your feelings clearly. Let her know that you consider her help to be an act of love. Emphasize that she is *giving* you something, not taking anything away. Emphasize that the *disease* will kill you, not the directives, not the decision she may be called upon to make.

It is natural to feel guilty about turning off respirators or other medical equipment. Many people say, "I want them to die naturally, not because the respirator was turned off." We forget that respirators are artificial. Feeding tubes are artificial. The most natural thing in the world is nature taking its course. Your proxy does not decide your death—*you* do. Your proxy only performs an act of love and mercy by ensuring that your wishes are respected.

Make sure your proxy has a copy of your Advanced Directives, and also give a copy to your doctor to place in your chart when you go to the hospital. Let your family know where they can find it quickly and easily. Bring your family together for a discussion early on in the disease process, or before you even get sick. Show them your Advanced Directives, let them hear your wishes clearly, and discuss their concerns. Discuss them now rather than over your hospital bed. It will be too late when you are in a coma, at which point *any* relative may insist that you be kept alive, and the doctors will have to keep the machines on. Afraid of being sued, the doctors will err on the side of doing too much rather than too little.

DOCTORS AND ADVANCED DIRECTIVES

A doctor may want you to stay "alive" because he'll feel he's failed if you die. Doctors may have been taught to fight to the bitter end, and they never have thought of death as the miracle that ends life, just as birth is the miracle that begins it. They may have been taught not to take verbal directives from an emotionally distraught relative. (Although who wouldn't be upset when a loved one is about to die?) They're worried about being hit with malpractice suits if they don't do everything conceivable to keep patients alive. And they don't want to get caught up in legal battles between family members. If even one relative says "keep him alive," doctors will follow the path of least legal danger and do so. Even a distant relative you haven't seen in twenty years can march into the hospital and tell the doctors to do everything possible to keep you alive.

Several years ago Heather received the phone call everyone dreads. Her father had suffered a heart attack and been rushed to the hospital. She quickly drove the two hours to be with him. When she found the doctor assigned to the case, who had never met her father before, she told him, "My father doesn't want any heroic measures."

Looking quite offended, the tall, gray-haired doctor replied: "I can't accept that, because I don't know that they are your father's wishes."

"I'm his daughter, his only relative," she replied. "I know what his wishes are."

"Do you have it in writing?" the doctor asked evasively.

Heather's father had signed an Advanced Directive, but she had forgotten to bring it. "Yes," she said, "but the paper is at my house."

"Well," he replied. "Until I see it, I can't assume it exists."

"I'm not leaving him for four hours to get it," she insisted, refusing to back down.

At this point the doctor grew defensive. "Can you prove you're his daughter?" the doctor demanded.

"In a flash!" she shouted back. "And do you really think I sneak into hospitals pretending to be some comatose guy's daughter just so I can pull the plug on him? This isn't about papers or ID. What's really going on?"

Having run out of dodges, the doctor admitted that, personally, he did not believe in letting people die. "I don't want my father to die either," Heather said softly, "but he's made it real clear that if he's going to end up on a respirator or be a vegetable, he wants nature to take its course. You're a complete stranger, you've never met my father before. Why should your belief system overrule ours?"

Before the doctor could reply, Heather continued: "You don't really care what my father wants, do you? You're fired! Send another doctor up right away. If you get anywhere near my father again, if you hinder his care, I'll call the police!"

Few confrontations are this dramatic or need to be. But if you and your doctor or loved one's doctor do not see eye to eye, it is appropriate to ask for another physician. It is your right. You can ask the nurses for recommendations or you can call the hospital administrator.

The care most people receive reflects their doctors' beliefs and values. It is crucial to establish a relationship with a physician who shares your values and beliefs. When we are treated by physicians whose values differ from ours, we're often talked into taking more or less aggressive measures than we would like to. It is vital to make your wishes known in Advanced Directives and to appoint a strong advocate to watch over you. Otherwise, you may find your control over the circumstances of your death slipping away from you.

POSITIVE OPTIONS

We have the right to participate in all decisions concerning our care, to set our own goals and to change them, and to expect honest and informative care. That kind of honesty harms no one. On the contrary, it can sometimes save their lives. Many patients literally beg to be "unplugged" and allowed to die not because they want to die but because they are in pain. When these patients understand the course of their diseases and the measures available to relieve or at least lessen their pain, many of them opt to continue living.

But doctors like to speak in negatives and they tend to withhold information. They also don't fully answer the questions put to them. They say what they *can't* do rather than what they can. They say that "nothing more can be done" instead of describing the many medicines and other therapies available for pain.

Even where there is no cure in sight, doctors can help people by speaking in the positive. When a disease becomes terminal they can say what they *can* do:

- ❊ *"We can provide aggressive comfort treatment."*
- ❊ *"We can set up a pain management program and reassess it constantly."*
- ❊ *"We can allow open visiting."*
- ❊ *"We can let you bring your pet."*
- ❊ *"We can let you have pizza."*
- ❊ *"We can improve the quality of the time you have remaining, making your last days or months as pleasant as possible."*
- ❊ *"We can let you participate in the ending phase of your life."*
- ❊ *"We can address your suffering and pain."*
- ❊ *"And when the time comes, we can manage your dying, just as you want it."*

You have the right to expect that kind of care, and if you don't get it, you have the right to initiate it.

4

THE PHYSIOLOGY OF PAIN

The right to be free of physical pain.
The right to be cared for by compassionate, sensitive,
  knowledgeable people who will attempt to under-
  stand one's needs.

Early one morning ten years ago I stood in a hospital corridor, dreading the sight I knew I would see when I pushed open the door and walked into Eric's room. It wasn't the blood I was afraid of, for there was none. Neither were there doctors rushing in and out of the room shouting orders, or machines whistling and beeping, or anguished relatives crying in the hallway and around the bed. It was absolutely silent and still in that room, and it was that utter silence that unnerved me.

Hospitals are lively and noisy in the morning: Breakfast is served; nurses check on their patients; doctors make their rounds; patients are taken from this department to that for tests; relatives come to visit. But in Room 601 at the end of the bustling corridor, everything was silent. The patient was alive, but he was afraid to move.

Inside of 601, Eric, a designer in his early thirties, was dying of AIDS. In addition to PCP (*Pneumocystis carinii* pneumonia), which often strikes people with AIDS, he was suffering from peripheral neuropathy, a disease that had destroyed the nerve endings in his arms and legs.

Peripheral neuropathy is a common complication of AIDS. For many it produces nothing more than an annoying tingling or numbness. But Eric wasn't so lucky. The disease destroyed the protective sheaths surrounding the nerves in his legs and feet, as well as in his hands and lower arms. Raw nerves were exposed, unprotected, leaving them extremely sensitive. The slightest movement of his legs, arms, feet, or hands, or even a shoulder movement that "pulled" on his arms, sent terrible pain messages screaming to his brain. "I can't even turn my neck," he whispered, moving his lips slowly and carefully. "It's like there are tight vises on my arms and legs, and someone keeps turning the screws," he said sorrowfully, fearfully. And so he lay in bed for weeks, as still as possible.

I've seen people screaming, crying, cursing, talking, yelling, begging, laughing, flailing, twitching, and writhing as they approach death. Never have I seen anyone so still. Of course, it was impossible for Eric to remain absolutely still. Every once in a while a doctor or nurse would touch him, or a muscle would twitch, and the silence would be shattered by his scream. But most of the time, it was absolutely quiet in Room 601. Even the sound on the heart monitor had been turned off because it distracted Eric.

Knowing that the end was near, I suggested to Eric's family and his partner, Scott, that they come to say their good-byes. We sat quietly by his bed that night, watching his face all night. His mother gently stroked his forehead but otherwise we didn't dare hold his hand or touch him. All we could do when he cried in pain was to cry ourselves. Early in the morning Eric died, as quiet and still as he had lived his last several weeks.

Finally able to touch and caress her son, Eric's mother put her head on his chest and cried. "I thought the pain when he was born was awful, but it was nothing like this," she sobbed. "The pain of watching your own child die in torture is devastating. To raise him all these years, to always hope for the best, and to see it end like this is more than I think I can handle. I couldn't feel his pain but I could see its effects. I felt so helpless, all I could do was stroke his forehead. I don't know if it helped, but it was all I could do. All I could do was be with him. I hoped and prayed for a miracle to put him out of his pain. He is now out of his pain. We were left in it."

Luckily, stories like Eric's are fewer and farther between as better pain management helps us to quell even the most stubborn pain.

Many people insist that they don't fear death, but they are terrified by the painful process of dying. Family and friends of the dying agree: Watching a loved one suffer is a horrible experience. Unfortunately, pain is a frequent companion at the end of life. Pain is our internal alarm system, telling us that something is wrong. It may alert us with a quiet whisper of pain. Other times, as patients have told me, the alarm is more like an "excruciating agony" or "torture." The pain alarm may be a helpful first warning, alerting us to danger. But in most cases the alarm rings often and needlessly as we approach death. Perhaps the alarm system is failing, short-circuiting. No one can say with certainty. And perhaps death, like birth, is simply a painful experience.

PAIN DEFINED

On a strictly physical level, pain is caused by impulses transmitted from specialized nerve receptors through the nerves to the spinal cord and brain. These impulses are messages telling of tissue damage, but there's more to pain than these messages. The damage the messages describe is interpreted and shaped in the brain, where the nerve impulses become what we experience as pain. How much the pain hurts and how we respond to it is due partially to our attitudes toward pain, and partially to our fears and past experiences with the sensation. Where and why the tissue damage is occurring also influences the type of pain we experience.

Pain can be sharp or dull, acute or chronic, continuous or intermittent, annoying or excruciating, stabbing, throbbing, distracting, shallow, or deep. It can limit itself to a little area or engulf the entire body. It is both physical and emotional. Pain may rush over us in an instant or creep into place so slowly that we don't notice it. It may come alone or bring with it nausea, fear, and other companions. Our reactions are as varied as the pain itself. Some people ask for help immediately. Others respond more subtly, only revealing their pain with a strained facial expression, a tense hand, or a sudden stiffening of the body. In some cases, we don't realize that people are in pain until they begin overreacting to stimuli, such as complaining about noise, light, bad food, or other things that were not bothersome before.

All pain is personal and subjective. The more you know about pain and how the medical system responds to it, the more effectively you can communicate and participate in managing your pain. The only one who knows how much it hurts is the person experiencing the pain. We can never truly know another's pain because we all respond to disease and trauma differently. We see pain through our eyes and our eyes only, our views filtered by our histories of pain and pain tolerance, as well as that of our culture. Since we can't measure or "prove" pain, we must always assume that it is very real, we must never discount or minimize it, and we must never dismiss it. Whether it is excruciating or mildly annoying, it is always very real to the person having it.

Sometimes pain distracts us, seeming to pull us away from life. In her final months, Cynthia seemed to be slipping into a world of her own, gradually withdrawing from life, spending more and more time in bed. At first we believed that this was a sign of impending death, for the dying can become very disengaged, letting go of the people and things of this world.

Cynthia consistently denied being in pain. She simply seemed to be thinking intently. "I just want to be left alone," she would say. And so we left her alone until I noticed that she grimaced as she tried to turn in bed. "Are you in pain?" I asked.

"No," she replied, dully.

I persisted. "Cynthia, it looked like trying to move hurt you."

She finally admitted that turning had been painful, so I asked her if we could try some pain medications just to help her turn. She agreed. Within hours she was up and around, more alert and interested in life than she had been in a long time. "I must have gotten used to the pain little by little," she said. "I knew I had just a little pain, but thought I could deal with it. Now that it's gone I see how much it had consumed me."

Cynthia's reaction to her pain was not unusual. We don't realize how much of our mind is utilized, how distracted we are by simple everyday problems such as a toothache or headache. Imagine how deeply fixated you could become with severe pain and how that might draw you entirely into yourself. Now try to imagine the amount of mental energy we might expend trying to deal with the pain of cancer or AIDS, the changes of old age, the fear of dying, et cetera. If a toothache is distracting, what happens when people are going through the biggest physical challenges of their lives? They may not even realize that the trance they are in is pain.

DYING AND PAIN

Dying is not always painful. Some patients with advanced cancer have reported feeling no pain as a result of their disease. An older person suffering from pneumonia may pass painlessly. There may be a great deal of anxiety as the ability to breathe diminishes, but if the right medications are given pain needn't be a problem. In fact, medical professionals often refer to pneumonia as the "older person's best friend" because it grants a quick, mostly pain-free death.

We can't prevent the physical pain of disease, but we can prevent unnecessary pain. We have numerous effective medications, and we have the right to use them to lessen the burden of disease. We don't "deserve" to hurt; we deserve to be free of pain as much as possible.

With modern pain-relieving agents available, *no one should have to live or die with pain*. Our medical providers have a duty to do all within their power to relieve pain, for the dying have the right to be free of pain. With proper medication and management, pain can be relieved most of the time. The Agency for Health Care Policy and Research, a branch of the U.S. Department of Health and Human Services, reported in 1994 that pain could be controlled in 90 percent of cancer patients. Unfortunately, too many people remain in pain: The same agency found that 42 percent of cancer patients received inadequate pain medication.

When I brought my father home to die, I promised him that he would be free of pain. With the arsenal of medications available through the doctors working with my company, and my home care experience and love, I felt I could guarantee that he would die in peace without any pain. But even with the best of care and concern, pain occasionally sneaks in, even if only for a few moments.

Two days before he died he had been doing well on small doses of morphine, enough to hold back the abdominal ache he felt as the cancer spread. Then, late at night, he was suddenly hit with what he called the worst pain of his life. He grabbed my arm with all the fury of his pain as he pleaded: "You promised me I wouldn't be in pain, you promised!" Only a few moments passed before the injection the nurse hurriedly administered began to take effect, but it seemed like an eternity. I felt miserable. I had failed my father. I made him a promise I couldn't keep, for I had forgotten what I had learned from other patients: Pain is part of the experience of dying.

Despite our assurances, and despite our most powerful medicines, our loved ones may suffer. Despite our fondest wishes, doctors cannot prevent *all* the pain of dying from occurring. Even in the best of all possible situations, some pain is inevitable.

In less than the best of all possible situations, pain must be endured. Sally, the attorney with uterine cancer who visited the cancer clinics in Tijuana, was pleased when she went into remission. But then the nurse from her doctor's office called to tell her that the latest testing had shown that the cancer was back. Within a few weeks it was clear that there was nothing more the doctors could do to check the disease, and her time was limited.

On a Friday morning, a bright and sunny Southern California morning, her family realized that she was rapidly getting worse. When her husband, Matthew, called the doctor's office to ask for help, a nurse told him that the doctor was unavailable. "My wife's not doing well," he told her, but she simply·repeated that the doctor was not available and suggested he take her to the emergency room. Sally's request was to die at home, surrounded by her family, lying in the bed she had shared with her husband for twenty-five years. Therefore, spending her last hours in a strange and sterile hospital room was not an option.

Sally lay that beautiful Friday day and evening at home, in her own bed, but in terrible pain. Late that night, a little past midnight, Matthew decided to call the doctor again. The doctor on call responded, saying that he was covering for the unavailable physician. "Can you give her some pain medicine?" Matthew asked. But this doctor said that he was unfamiliar with the case and didn't feel comfortable prescribing anything having not examined Sally. "Bring her to the office on Monday, or I'll meet you at the emergency room in one hour."

Still, Sally wanted to die at home, the home she and Matthew had bought with such excitement when they were young, the home she had lovingly decorated, the home where they had raised their children and entertained their friends. "I'm going to die soon," she whispered to her family when they suggested that she change her mind and go to the emergency room. "I don't want to die in an ambulance on the way to the hospital. I'd rather die here." And she did die there, in her home, early Saturday morning.

Sally's death was inevitable, but her suffering was not. Her husband could have easily been taught to give her a few simple injections, or a nurse could have been sent to set up an intravenous drip of pain medicine. She was under the care of an oncologist, she had a caring family and plenty of money to pay for any service and medicine necessary, and she lived within thirty minutes' driving time of two major, world-renowned medical centers. Yet she died in pain, despite all this.

Sally's pain was exacerbated by her decision to die at home. Many in our medical system don't know what to do with the dying. If Sally had asked for another MRI or surgery, the doctors and nurses would have known exactly what to do, and it would have been handled smoothly. But Sally wanted to die at home, in peace.

If you find yourself in a situation like this, clearly explain to the nurse that your loved one is in pain and needs medication. You may have to insist on speaking to the doctor. If the doctor is not available, ask to speak to one of his associates, or look in your local phone book under nursing or hospice services; many of them specialize in pain management. (These companies can often expedite a call to your doctor, and if your doctor is unavailable, they typically have their own physicians on call for just such emergencies.) Do not take no for an answer. Pain may, at times, be unavoidable, but suffering should never be an option.

UNNECESSARY PAIN

Although pain is a part of the death process, there is an arsenal of pain medicines with which to quell it. But even in hospitals, surrounded by brilliant physicians and dedicated nurses, too many of the dying are still not given enough medicine. The problem is that there are rules. Patients and their families and friends are puzzled and frustrated by nurses who say that no more medicines can be given until such-and-such time.

Exasperated, an elderly woman named Beverly once shouted at me when I was arranging her transfer from the hospital to home care: "My pain medicine is on a strict schedule, but my pain isn't! My cancer isn't! I don't hurt exactly every four hours. I hate having to wait that last half-hour until three o'clock. That's when I can finally get my shot—but the nurses are changing shift and everyone's busy. Don't they care?"

Nurses care, but they often don't understand how you are feeling. That's why constant reassessment of your pain is suggested. A patient's pain and the efficacy of treatment should be continually monitored. Pain should be assessed:

🎴 *At regular intervals*

🎴 *With each new report of pain*

🎴 *At suitable intervals after each pharmacological intervention, such as fifteen to thirty minutes after parenteral drug therapy (given in another form other than by mouth) and one hour after oral administration.*

Health care professionals should ask about the pain, and the patient's response or complaint should be listened to carefully. The "ABCDE" approach to pain assessment is simple and effective:

A. **A**sk about pain regularly.
B. **B**elieve the patient and family in their reports of pain and what relieves it.

C. **C**hoose pain control options appropriate for the patient, family, and setting.

D. **D**eliver interventions in a timely, logical, and coordinated fashion.

E. **E**mpower patients and their families.

People often complain that their doctors seem to be so stingy with pain medicines and hardened to patients' pain. There are many reasons why physicians undermedicate. Often they simply don't know enough about pain. Doctors are taught very little about pain in school, and most have not undergone the terrible pain of cancer or other diseases themselves. Most doctors who undergo painful illnesses become more sensitive to their patients' pain. Some believe that it's a patient's duty to keep a stiff upper lip, or think that the patient is faking pain in order to get drugs. But for the most part, doctors are afraid of addicting their patients to strong narcotics. They are afraid of giving too much medicine, and they are afraid of being sued.

THE FEAR OF ADDICTION

Doctors worry about patients becoming addicted to powerful painkilling drugs, as do many patients and their families. But the fear of addiction is largely unjustified. The number of people who actually become addicted is small, some believe as small as 1 percent. One study concluded that "Most patients with cancer take opioids (analgesics such as morphine, codeine, methadone) for more than two weeks, and only very rarely do they exhibit the drug abuse behaviors and psychological dependence that characterize addiction." Still the fear of addiction is great because the results can be serious when it does happen.

This is especially true early on in a disease process. I have seen people waste the valuable time they had remaining by becoming fixated on a drug that they have been given prematurely or one that has a rapid tolerance and had to be given more and more often or in larger and larger doses. I saw it happen to Kevin, the thirty-five-year-old artist, as he lay dying at home. Kevin was a true lover of life. You could "read" his happiness in his paintings, you could hear it in his voice, you could see it in his laughing eyes. When he was first diagnosed with lymphoma, Kevin said to me: "As I round the last corner I won't hang on unreasonably, I'll let nature take its course. But until then, until the last second, I'm living life all the way! Why not spend every minute possible with my family, friends, and pets?"

Several months later, Kevin developed a severe chronic pain, for which he was given Demerol. Like morphine, Dilaudid, Tylenol, Advil, and aspirin, Demerol is a short-acting medicine. Unfortunately, Demerol is a poor choice for chronic pain because patients tend to quickly develop a tolerance for the drug. Kevin became not only addicted but also fixated on the Demerol. He paid little attention to his family and friends and his beloved pets. All he could do was think about his next dose, watching the clock as the minute hand moved agonizingly slowly. One night, everyone in the house was scared out of their wits as the house erupted in noise: tables and chairs were being knocked over, dishes pulled out of cupboards, drawers yanked out and dropped to the ground. They rushed into the kitchen to find Kevin, in a sweaty, frantic rage, searching for the Demerol they had hidden from him. When he saw them he fell to the floor in tears. "I can't believe this has become my life," he cried. "This is not how I wanted it to end."

Kevin's addiction was squeezing the quality out of the ending phase of his life. He was quickly taken off the Demerol and put on a less addictive, longer-acting pain reliever, enabling him to enjoy several weeks of real quality with his loved ones. (Longer-acting pain relievers include the morphine derivative MS Contin, Roxanol, and methadone.)

Addiction is a valid concern in the early and middle stages of a disease, but the problem becomes less important in the final stages of life. Many doctors feel that it doesn't matter if someone who will probably die in a matter or hours, days, weeks, or months becomes addicted. If against all expectations they're cured, if they live, they can then worry about breaking their habits.

If a family continues to fear addiction when death is perhaps a few breaths away, they are probably in denial, focusing on an imagined addiction rather than facing the reality of impending death. Addiction certainly interferes with our life psychologically, but we should not let this fact interfere with our need to control physical pain. There is a time to worry about addiction, and a time to make our loved ones comfortable. The two should not be confused.

FEAR OF MORPHINE

Some people are not worried about addiction. Rather, they fear that pain relievers may knock them out, incapacitate them, or reduce their ability to think. The bigger problem is untreated pain, which by itself may rob us of our mental faculties. Pain can fill our consciousness, blotting out everything else.

Christopher, a thirty-five-year-old realtor, decided to go on morphine during the last stage of an extended, losing battle with lymphoma. He had resisted taking the narcotic for a long time, but finally the pain was too great.

Morphine can be given by mouth, injection, or intravenously (IV). In this case, the IV route was most appropriate. Christopher asked his family to gather round before he took the first dose of the medicine. One at a time they said good-bye to him, their son, brother, and cousin. Everyone's eyes were filled with tears as the drug began to drip from the IV bag hung on the pole by his bedside into his arm. Christopher took a big breath and closed his eyes as he felt his pain subsiding. His family stood by, silent and sad, waiting for the end.

Five minutes passed. No one had moved, said a word, or even coughed. Then Christopher's eyes opened and a look of embarrassment flooded his face. "I'm not dead," he said, almost regretfully. "I thought I'd be dead by now."

"Why?" I asked.

"Because I thought taking the morphine meant it was all over," he replied sheepishly. And suddenly everyone present howled with laughter, partially in relief and partially because his reaction to remaining alive was so funny. Christopher did not die that day. He went on to live for quite a while after his "big exit."

Like Christopher, many people believe that morphine is only given to those about to die. (Perhaps they remember, from their childhood, the elderly relative who was given morphine while dying, so they associate the drug with death.) If I don't take it, they tell themselves, I won't die. Morphine is an excellent pain reliever at the end stage of life. But it is not, in itself, the end or the reason for the end. People die from a disease, not from morphine. I have often heard doctors say to hesitant patients: "Let's try it. If at some point you no longer need it, we can discontinue it. If it doesn't work or it's just not for you, then we will try something else." I try to remind them they are in control of it, not the other way around.

THE FIVE RULES OF MEDICATION

The medical aspects of pain are shrouded in misunderstandings, incomplete knowledge, fear, and legalities. That's why it's important for patients, as well as their families and friends, to know what doctors and nurses are thinking when they are asked for help with pain.

Early in their training, health professionals are taught five Rules of Medication:

❧ *The Right Drug*

❧ *The Right Patient*

❧ *The Right Dose*

❧ *The Right Time*

❧ *The Right Route*

The Right Drug—Many drugs, some with similar-sounding names, are used to control pain. Each drug has different effects and side effects, so it is vital that patients receive the one(s) prescribed by the doctor, and no others. Taking someone else's medicine can be dangerous, for it may interact in a negative way with other drugs you are taking, or may be the wrong type of medication for your pain. If you have old medicines, or some that a friend gave you, show them to your doctor. He or she will either explain why it won't work in your case, or let you know if it is still potent, safe, and effective. (Most doctors understand that medications can be costly, and are willing to let you use medicines you already have, or get from a friend, if they have a chance to examine and evaluate it.)

Health professionals are also concerned about problems with multiple drugs. Many patients are on several medications that may be taken at different times of the day, increasing the opportunity for mistakes. That's why nurses are trained to carefully check before administering any medicines, and to administer only those that have been prescribed.

The Right Patient—Many patients and their loved ones are upset or frightened when a nurse repeatedly asks their names or checks the name bands on their wrists. "Don't they know who we are by now?" they wonder. The nurses may know who you are, but they cannot risk giving medicine to the wrong patient. That's why the careful nurse checks each and every time.

The Right Dose—To ensure that a medicine works effectively, with minimum side effects, it must be given in the right dose. We generally begin with the lowest effective dose, and if that is not enough we gradually increase the dose. The cause of the pain, the patient's general health, history, pain tolerance, and weight are all considered when determining the right dose. Since overdosing is a legitimate concern, many doctors and nurses prefer to underprescribe rather than overprescribe, waiting for a strong request before giving more. I am sure this makes a lot of sense if you are not the one in pain, but it is terrible when someone has to ask over and over again or cry or plead for pain relief.

The Right Time—Most pain medications are given every four to six hours. Some are longer-acting and may be given every eight or more hours. Medications may also be ordered "p.r.n.," the abbreviation for the Latin *pro re nata*, which means "as needed." A "p.r.n." medication is given only if requested by the patient and if she states that she is in pain.

Unfortunately, medicines don't relieve pain from the moment they enter the body until the second they wear off. Instead, they are most effective in the middle periods, after they've "gathered their strength" and before they've begun to "tire out" as the medicine is metabolized by the liver. This means that patients may continue feeling the pain for some time after the medicine is given and feel it returning before it's time for the next dose. This waxing and waning makes pain control uneven. New devices such as the portable IV pumps are being used to keep a consistent and effective amount of medicine in the bloodstream.

Pain is easiest to control at the onset and hardest at its peak. That's why it's best to ask for help *before* the pain becomes too severe.

It is now suggested that medications for persistent cancer-related pain should be administered on a round-the-clock basis, with additional as-needed doses. This helps to maintain a constant level of the drug in the body, and helps to prevent a recurrence of pain.

The Right Route—Medications may be given by mouth—pills, oral suspensions, or sublingual (under the tongue), intramuscular or subcutaneous injections (shots), suppository (rectally), transdermal (skin patch), or by intravenous injection (IV into a vein). Taking medications by mouth is obviously the easiest way. But many times, medications cannot be swallowed. They may be poorly absorbed in the stomach or cause gastrointestinal problems such as nausea, vomiting, and constipation. And many times patients can't take pills or liquids because they have difficulty swallowing or are already suffering from nausea or vomiting caused by their diseases. When the pain is great, medicine may be injected directly into the bloodstream.

Narcotic painkillers are often injected, but shots require repeated skin puncturing and the pain control is uneven. You'll feel relief some time after getting the shot, when the medicine has built up in the body. But then the pain returns as the liver begins to metabolize the drug. That's why an IV, which allows small amounts of medicine to drip into the body over a long period of time, usually becomes the method of choice as the disease progresses. Many patients resist the IV at first because they feel it is too permanent or only for the very ill or because it decreases their mobility. They rapidly come to appreciate the effectiveness of an IV, however, and do not miss the repeated pricks of a shot. In some cases, patients are given "pumps" which allow them to control the amount of medicine flowing from their IV into their body. With built-in safeguards, the patient can control and respond to his or her own pain without depending on others. The preference for IVs may change, however, for there is a growing movement in hospice favoring easy-to-administer sublingual and oral medication whenever possible over IVs.

RELIEVING PAIN: WHAT YOU CAN DO

We will probably all endure pain at some point in our lives. We need not, however, be victims of pain, or watch helplessly as our loved ones suffer. There are many things we can do for ourselves and for others.

❁ *Communicate clearly about your pain. Tell your doctors:*

　❁ *How it hurts—the pain is stabbing, hot, sharp, dull, prickly, aching*

- *How much it hurts—using words like "mild," "moderate," and "severe," or rating your pain on a scale of 1 to 10. Pain scales are an effective way of communicating and evaluating pain.*

- *Exactly where it hurts—naming or pointing to a specific location.*

- *When it hurts—constantly, intermittently, only after meals, when I turn over, it hits all at once, it sneaks up on me.*

- *Ask for a pain-control plan that spells out what medicines you will receive, when, and why. This will not only force your doctor to spend time thinking about controlling your pain, it will also reduce your anxiety. Ask about the frequency and whether it matches the way your pain occurs. Ask what will happen if the medication fails to control the pain: Will they increase the dosage or try a different medicine? Ask what you can do if the pain is uncontrollable in the middle of the night or on the weekend.*

- *Educate your doctor and nursing staff on your pain history. Tell them, if you know, whether you have a high or low tolerance for pain and which medications have or have not worked for you in the past. Let them know if you're quick to ask for relief or if you have difficulty doing so. When I asked Dr. James Thommes, a respected oncologist and AIDS physician, about pain, he replied, with irony: "I don't recommend it. That's why I tell patients to bring their doctors up to speed about their pain." If your doctor does not share your views on pain relief, get one who does. Look for a doctor who is able to give you compassionate care, which in itself is a great pain reliever.*

- *Don't be a martyr or a silent sufferer. Complain if you are in pain. Be vocal. Don't take no for an answer. If your doctor is not available, demand to see another. If your doctor will not help you control your pain, find another. This is harder to do if you have managed care, but you can try. Don't worry that people won't like you anymore. Passivity and pain relief do not go well together.*

❧ *Be proactive—and vocal—when fighting pain. There are still many health care professionals who frown upon the use of narcotics and others who are simply not experienced enough to know what kind and how much pain control is needed. If you or your loved one is in pain, speak up. Be forceful. Request a pain management consultation—demand it, if need be.*

❧ *Remember that our modern medical system doesn't function well on weekends. If you are having any pain on Friday, try not to wait to call the doctor until the pain becomes unbearable at midnight on Saturday. Be prepared. Ask your doctor to prepare a plan, and to leave orders for pain control on the weekend or at nights, when he or she is hard to find.*

❧ *Look into alternative means of controlling pain. Some people use prayer, some meditation, others use visualization—imagining themselves on a beautiful beach in Hawaii, looking up at the blue sky. Others visualize the inside of their bodies, watching as their own endorphins knock out the pain. Endorphins are chemicals produced in the brain which have pain-reducing effects similar to morphine. Any method that works for you is worthwhile. There are many excellent books on alternatives, as well as audiotapes and videotapes.*

❧ *Arrange to have a loved one with you as much as possible. Pain can make us feel isolated, completely alone. Sometimes, simply knowing that you are not alone is helpful. A tender hand to hold or a loving voice to listen to is a special kind of a medicine.*

Susan, a social worker, has seen pain and death many times. But none of her experiences with the last phase of life were as deep or lasting as her mother's death.

Esther, her mother, developed colon cancer. The large-boned seventy-two-year-old, who retained hints of her past grandeur, was in constant pain during the last months of her life. But pain seemed to bring out the best in Esther, a woman who had already suffered greatly. When she was only sixteen years old she had watched her own mother die of cancer.

"Mother was very dignified about her pain," Susan told me. "This was so surprising from a woman who had trouble with the catsup bottle breaking. She never lost her sense of humor. She would say that she was so sick, she wouldn't buy fruit that wasn't ripe."

It was toughest in those moments that the injections began to wear off or the pain would suddenly intensify. Susan couldn't make her mother's pain go away, so she just sat with her. They talked, they cried, they laughed. In the end, Susan and the rest of her family took shifts around the clock, making sure that Esther was never alone.

Finally the mother said to the daughter: "I can't take the pain anymore."

"Then don't," Susan answered. "It's okay for you to go."

Susan knew that sometimes there's nothing you can do but be there. She did not want her mother to die either, but she didn't want her mother to be in such pain any longer.

If you've done everything you can to help control your loved one's pain, you can simply be there. If she needs to cry, let her. Cry with her. Sharing tears is better than holding them in. Let her hold your hand, let her squeeze it when the pain hits. If she needs to scream, let her. Don't tell her that she's upsetting other patients or giving in to her pain. Let her scream, encourage her to scream, scream *with* her if you need to. Laugh with her, if you can.

At the very end, when there's nothing more to do, just say "I can't stop your pain, I can't make it go away. All I can do is sit here. So I'll sit here. Someone who loves you will sit here and hold your hand to the end. You won't be alone."

PAIN AS PUNISHMENT

Though pain may be loud or quiet, long or brief, cruel or merciful, it is never a punishment. Still, the idea of pain as a penalty haunts us, perhaps because our word "pain" comes from the Greek word *poine,* which means penalty. Family members are often horrified when their parents or spouses or children or siblings suffer through painful deaths. "I can't believe he is having pain," they'll say in anguish. "He led such a good life." "She never hurt anyone, why is she in so much pain?" "How can God allow this?"

Pain is no one's fault. I've witnessed hundreds of deaths without once seeing any correlation between the pain suffered and the person's goodness or evilness. Pain is often a part of death, just as it is an accompaniment to birth. Good people don't always die quietly in their sleep or pass painlessly. Nice people suffer just as much as not-so-nice people. Pain is not a judgment. It is simply a part of many people's last days, weeks, or months on earth.

Susan, who told her mother that it was okay to pass on rather than continue to endure pain, got a call from the hospital that night at 2 A.M., telling her that her mother had suffered a heart attack. As Susan drove to the hospital, hoping her mother's pain would not continue, she looked up and saw a shooting star. "I knew it was okay," she later told me, "I knew she was gone. Gone from the pain, gone from the suffering." Many years have passed, and Susan is now in her fifties. With eyes that are still teary, she says, "I never stopped missing her. But she's out of her pain."

THE LESSONS OF PAIN

Pain is a great equalizer, making us softer and more empathetic. Marianne Williamson tells the story of a woman who went to a dinner party. There she met a terribly angry man from whom everyone shied away. When the man told her that he had just had a cancer operation, she decided to sit next to him. They had a great time talking to each other that evening, and she felt that they had really connected, despite his anger. Six months earlier she'd had a serious health scare herself, making her as fearful then as she knew the man was now. The woman felt that it was her personal responsibility to sit with the angry man rather than to run from him.

Pain can give insight into other people's fears, it can give us the empathy to care, and it can give us the desire to help. Pain deepens our ability to feel and our experience of life. We struggle to avoid suffering but from it our eyes and ears open wider to the pain of others. Having been hurt, we better understand others' pain.

Every pain has a purpose, even the pain that accompanies death. That pain helps us die; it makes the suit of clothes we call our body no longer habitable. We hang on to life as long as we possibly can, clinging to the essence and identity of our body. We can detach from all that we have known only if pushed to do so by a powerful force. Pain may be the force that helps us to separate and let go of life. For some, it is the push that makes us leap out into the unknown. I have seen many people full of fight, determined to live, who changed their minds only when their bodies filled with pain. Some say, "I don't know what is next, but it has to be better than this pain." For those in pain, death is a comfort.

I've told many loved ones the story of the ancient king who asked his advisers for something to help him get through the good times and the bad times. Many came forth with potions and armor, but his magician gave him a simple ring. Inside the ring, the words "This too shall pass" had been inscribed.

When you're watching a loved one in pain, time passes in the slowest possible motion. Although it seems unending and unendurable, all pain eventually ends. If you've done everything you can and your loved one is still in pain, remember that you can go a long way with a tear and a smile. This too shall pass.

5

THE EMOTIONS OF PAIN

*The right to express feelings and emotions about pain
in one's own way.*

Hospitals are filled with negative feelings: anger, depression, agitation, anxiety, hostility, nervousness, and fear. Many of these feelings stem from pain—the physical pain of disease and the emotional pain generated by the fear of dying, which is made worse by the physical pain. Patients tend to respond either by striking out in anger or withdrawing in depression. Anger is a cry of rage against fate and a plea for help. Depression is another way of responding to the same pain. Many people look for quick answers that will instantly relieve the pain, but ultimately the only way out of the pain is through the pain.

Angry, pained, and undermedicated, the elderly cancer patient Beverly, who had complained that her pain wasn't on a schedule, continued to make life miserable for the hospital staff. "Watch out," they warned one another, "she'll rip your head off for no reason." Beverly argued with her doctors, screamed at the nurses, intimidated the orderlies, threw her food trays on the floor, and left many volunteers in tears. She was even nasty to her own family—so nasty, they came to visit her as little as possible. Her daughter vowed not to bring the grandchildren by anymore because all Beverly did was bark at them.

Several nurses warned me when I first came to discuss her case. "Watch out for her," they said. "She is a real witch."

I've seen this happen many times. Although health care professionals are taught not to label patients, they do. A patient may be in a bad mood one day, perhaps because he just received the unhappy diagnosis, or maybe because he's in pain. Whatever the reason, he finds himself labeled "angry" or "prone to agitation" or a "jerk" when he snaps at a nurse. The next shift of nurses hears this and tries to avoid the patient as much as possible. Upon learning that the man is a "problem," the doctors decide to keep their visits brief and perfunctory, which only upsets the frightened patient even more. The cycle continues, leaving the patient isolated, scared, and more angry than ever.

Some patients become quiet and depressed rather than angry. We tend to disapprove of depression, for we think it means that someone has given up on life. Doctors and nurses often say "that patient is depressed" as if it were a bad thing.

Depression is a natural reaction for someone faced with life-challenging illness, someone in terrible pain who is contemplating saying good-bye to everything he or she has ever known and loved. Yet, we're as afraid of depression as we are of anger. We shun it and we try to help people "snap out of it." Better to let people sit with their depression, accept it, give it time, pay it attention, and let it take its natural course. It cannot be "fixed" or banned.

Of course the dying are depressed. Lying in bed, faced with a life-challenging illness, we lose most everything: our physical health and strength and our ability to take care of ourselves. Nurses measure our urine and help us to the bathroom, challenging our dignity. We lose our dreams for the future. We lose the chance to watch our children or grandchildren kick a goal on the soccer field, graduate from school, get married, have children, and grow old. All we have left are our feelings and emotions. Whether we're anxious, fearful, withdrawn, depressed, hostile, or nervous, those reactions are ours. We have a right to express them.

THE FEAR OF PAIN

"Can you know the things I imagine every time a new pain hits?" Beverly asked me. "Every single time I wonder why I'm hurting: Is the cancer getting worse? Is there a new tumor? Did the chemotherapy fail again? Are the drugs wearing off? Did they give me the right medicine? Am I becoming immune to it? Will the nurses come when I ring the bell? Will they give me something or tell me that I've got to wait two hours for the next dose? Will they believe me or just think I'm a complainer? Every pain hurts more than just physically."

It is natural to fear pain. We fear that the doctors won't be able to relieve our pain. We fear that it will be out of control, overwhelming, and excruciating. We fear that we won't be able to handle the pain. We fear that we'll cry and look like wimps and whiners.

In all my years of treating terminally ill patients, I have never seen one who was not fearful at some point. Pain is stressful. Being in a hospital is stressful. Facing a life-threatening illness is stressful. Put all three together and the inevitable result is fear. And fear makes pain worse.

Pain is inextricably bound up with fear. Mild fear, which

we call anxiety, can keep us on edge and preoccupy our minds. Anxiety heightens the feeling of pain and builds to outright fear. If you're both pained and fearful, doctors and nurses may want to medicate you less or they'll try sedation to relieve your fear. They may be reluctant to give you more pain medicine, no matter how much you need it, or they may discount your pain, thinking that your problem is emotional not physical.

Try to get your doctors to address the emotion itself. Antianxiety medicines have their place, but they're just one tool and not necessarily the first. It's best to begin reducing fear of pain by educating the patient, explaining why the pain is occurring, how it's going to be handled, what kind of pain control will be offered and when, what to do if the pain strikes in the middle of the night, what will happen if the plan fails, and what other options are available. Detailed explanations reduce anxiety by reassuring the patient that he or she will not be left alone to suffer.

Distraction also helps relieve anxiety and fear. Conversation, listening to the radio, watching television, playing games with a friend, and having someone tell you the latest jokes can take your mind off your pain, if only for a little while. Author Norman Cousins watched old films as part of his own treatment for a serious disease. We can't be sure if distraction and entertainment work on a psychological level by possibly reducing the anxiety and fear which are thought to worsen pain, or on a physical level by spurring the release of endorphins and perhaps other substances that may block pain. Perhaps it works on both levels, simultaneously.

Deep breathing, prayer, meditation, visualization, and similar practices are very helpful. I remember working with a man in deep pain, telling him to "breathe into the pain." He quickly snapped back, "How about if I breathe into getting a bat and hitting you on the head?"

"After you have your bat and breathe into hitting me," I continued, not sure whether he was serious or was kidding, "what would you do to the pain with the bat?"

He explained in great detail how he would smash the pain with the bat, how he would beat the pain senseless and rip it to shreds. The exercise actually helped lessen his pain. It gave him a sense of power in a situation in which he had felt powerless. Power and control are important factors in pain, for patients feel that they will lose control of their health, of their bodies, of their ability to think and take care of themselves, of their ability to relate to others. They fear that they will be powerless and out of control. That's one reason why education, distraction, entertainment, prayer, deep breathing, meditation, and visualization are helpful: They give us a sense of control over our pain.

Reassurance is vital. I've found that it's best to emphasize that everything is under control. When patients ask about their pain, I'll often say something like: "This is the medicine you'll be given. We've had good results with it before. We're confident that it will work. If it doesn't control your pain or has side effects, we have many other medicines for you. And if your pain intensifies, we can increase the dosage. We have many ways to take care of your pain. We'll do whatever it takes."

And sometimes you can't educate, distract, or reassure a loved one struggling with physical and emotional pain. Sometimes all you can do is let them squeeze your hand. And that, by itself, is a great pain reliever.

ANGER AND DEPRESSION

Hurting, frightened, feeling as if they've lost control over life and are at the mercy of a very cruel fate, patients may turn on their family, friends, doctors, and nurses, screaming, snapping, insulting, and pushing everyone away. When a patient rages inappropriately we tend to draw back, back down, hurry away, avoid trouble. Family members cut visits short. Doctors and nurses do only what is absolutely necessary. It's very easy for us to judge or dismiss this anger. It's more difficult to explore it.

I've often asked angry patients why they're mad. At first they complain about the lousy food or the uncaring staff, about how much the last shot hurt or the crummy television reception. Beverly, the furious woman with cancer, gave me a similar litany of complaints. I listened with compassion, then asked her to go on and tell me more about her rage. "I'm angry because I hurt so much and because everyone hates me," she cried out. "I'm angry because I'm dying, and I'm angry because I am all alone!"

When someone rages in anger, the best thing we can do is to listen. This is the moment to ask them about their pain or fear. This is the time to tell them that we wish we could make everything all better for them. We can't cure their disease, erase their pain, or quiet their fears, but we can listen. Being heard sometimes relieves pain; it almost always dissipates anger.

Remember that anger often comes from pain and that anger directed toward you is not about you. You're just a convenient target. If you can understand this, you can help relieve the pain by sharing it. Be prepared, however: Your loved one may push you away when you first approach. If it happens, let it happen, but be with the person anyway. John Bradshaw talks about separating but staying connected. Take a break, then come back. If you can't visit, call. If you can be with them, if you can understand their anger and listen to them, you *are* helping.

Anger is socially taboo, yet studies have shown over and over again that angry patients live longer. Whether they do so because they externalize their feelings or because they demand more pain relief, and more care, we don't know. We do know that anger creates action. Anger helps us control the world around us. If the anger is not inappropriate, violent, or abusive, it is a sometimes helpful response, one that should not be stifled.

Many depressed people withdraw from life, responding less vocally and visibly to their pain. Doctors and nurses often react to this by giving less pain medication, because the patient isn't complaining as much anymore. The medical system is good at medicating noisy patients who complain but not people who remain quiet. The sadness and mourning of depression are a natural response to disease and pain. The way to lift the depression is to work through the grief, take time to mourn the loss of our health and mobility, and be saddened by what has now maybe become a daily fight with pain.

When, however, someone wishes to shake their depression but cannot, antidepressant medications may be necessary. These medicines can help to lift one out of what seems to be a bottomless depression. Antidepressants are a useful adjunct to other pain control measures in raising the pain threshold.

Treating depression is a balancing act: We must accept sadness as an appropriate, natural stage of dying without letting an unmanaged, ongoing depression subtract from the quality of life. Depression may be optimally managed by using a combination of support, psychotherapy, and antidepressant medications. You and your physician can find the approach that is best for you.

APPROPRIATE FEELINGS

Other people are uncomfortable when they see us in pain. They may be upset because they don't want to see us suffer. They may be upset because we are not expressing our distress in the "proper" way. They might like us to respond to our pain politely, stoically, or with only a modest hint of discomfort in the voice to prove that the pain is real. They certainly do not want us screaming and cursing or being embarrassing or disruptive. Screaming and yelling are normal responses to pain. I'm more surprised when people don't scream and holler when they're in excruciating pain, but we've been thoroughly trained not to give voice to our "bad" feelings.

Your loved ones, your doctors, and your nurses may not like how you feel your pain or how you express it, but it's your pain and you have a right to express your feelings and emotions about it in your own way. When you're facing a life-threatening and painful illness you may feel angry, depressed, fearful, anxious, outraged, or terrified. Whatever you feel, your feelings are correct and you are entitled to them.

Even feeling nothing is proper. Joseph, a colleague of mine and a physician, once called after learning that his uncle had cancer of the lungs, bone, and pancreas. "I expected to have a huge emotional reaction," the puzzled doctor said, "but I felt nothing. All I can do is talk to my relatives intellectually about his situation. My uncle has meant so much to me, I don't understand why I am not feeling more."

We feel our feelings when they hit us, not when we think we should. Joseph is a very caring and compassionate man. Perhaps he was still in shock. Perhaps he would have another reaction when he visited his uncle in the hospital. Perhaps he was simply too uncomfortable with "bad" feelings to allow himself to experience them at all. I reminded Joseph of his love and compassion, telling him that he would cry when he was ready to and that the time when he finally cried would be the right time.

Numbness, denial, and withdrawal are all appropriate reactions, for the moment. They will make way for other emotions at the right time, but not before. Rather than sort through our feelings to find the "right" one, it's better to simply let them wash over us, in their own time. When I discussed Joseph's case with Elisabeth Kübler-Ross, she said in her simple and profound way: "What you're feeling is what you're feeling. Don't judge it, just let it be."

Elisabeth has shared with me how painful this last year has been for her. She's ready to die, but she is not dying—nor is she getting well. My place as a friend is to allow her her feelings, to listen and to be there for her. I bring her things to read, favorite foods, and hopefully, some good companionship. She herself has often said that if you're still here, it is for a purpose.

Feelings sometimes are overwhelming. If you are feeling as if you cannot go on because a loved one is dying, it's okay to take a break or get help.

There is a surprising amount of help available. There are support groups for people facing life-challenging illness, for people with cancer or AIDS, as well as groups for family, friends, and significant others. Many of these groups are listed in your local telephone book. You can always speak to a hospital minister, priest, rabbi, or social worker, who are excellent resources. Your doctor or therapist can also help you through your emotional stress.

People at their wits' end have often said: "I thought about taking a Xanax or something to help me calm down, but decided I shouldn't." They say that they don't want to take drugs, that they "did that in college," or that they "don't take drugs for fun." Drugs may certainly be overused, but there *is* an appropriate time for medicine, and dealing with death is just the time for which many medications were created. Unless you have a history of addiction, it's all right to look for help from appropriate medications at a moment of overwhelming sorrow or anxiety.

If you're numb with shock, that's all right. If you're furious, if you're outraged, if you're sad, if you're crazed, or if you need help, that's all right too. *All* of your feelings are appropriate.

THE PAIN OF LOSS

Emotional pain can be just as hard as physical pain. There is no heartbreak worse than the pain of permanent, seemingly senseless separation from those we dearly love. So far, at least, there are no medicines to treat that sorrow.

The pain of loss can be sharp, shattering our control and thrusting our jagged edges to the surface. It can be deadening, dulling our senses and taking away our joy. It can be paralyzing, robbing us of the will to go on living. Whatever form it takes, the pain hurts terribly. If we are dying, we have to find a way to say good-bye to all we have known, loved, and cherished. If we are witnessing the end of life, we have to find a way to survive the pain of losing a loved one.

Physical pain is easy to see. If a woman walked into the room with her arm bleeding, we would all stop and give her the attention she needs. But emotional pain is difficult to see, and even harder to understand if it's "old." When someone says that a dear friend was killed in a car accident a few years ago, we don't really stop and take note. But if we could go back to that terrible moment and see what happened to the friend, we would understand it on a new, deeper level.

In counseling at a deathbed, I am always aware of how intense the pain is, how close it is to the surface. Often, all I have to say to someone is, "I see you are in a lot of pain," and they let it out. Others will talk about it briefly, then move on to something else. If I feel strongly something was avoided or left unsaid, I will go back to the pain. Usually, however, I move on to a new topic. The pain can be so great, so over-whelming, that it can only be touched a little at a time.

The only way out of the pain is through the pain. Resisting or refusing to face pain simply delays the inevitable and adds to the grief. We may not want to face the pain, or feel it, but it won't disappear. We can defer it, but only at the cost of prolonging the problem. That's why it's better to go through the events as they occur, responding openly and honestly to everything that happens. Talk to someone about your pain, whether it be physical or emotional. Hold some-one's hand and cry. It may scare you. It may feel as if your finger is in a dike and a terrible flood of pain will rush over you if you let that finger slip. It may feel that way, yes, but you will survive, you will continue, you will move on. Whatever happens, don't turn away from the pain. We're stronger than we think, and we're never given more than we can handle.

If you do put off facing your pain, if you do deny it, forgive yourself. If you're not feeling anything now, if you can't allow yourself to let go, so be it. You're not alone. Your pain will find you at a later date, and you can deal with it then. Children who lose their parents often defer their pain for years. We cannot take away the pain that death causes, but if we experience it fully, we can prevent the wounding that so many people feel when pain is not dealt with as it occurs.

BEYOND THE PAIN

I spent an afternoon talking with Beverly, the woman who had been branded a "problem." We spoke about the cancer that was destroying her bones, we spoke of her fear of pain, and we spoke of death. We discussed the various pain medicines she might use, injections, IVs, biofeedback, acupuncture, and everything else she wanted to talk about. She told me that she had grown up on the banks of the Mississippi, that she had been the first woman in her family and in her town to attend college, and that she had married Hank, "the handsomest man in the county." In their twenty years together they had built a family, a home, and a business. When he died, she took him "back to the water" and buried him as close to the Mississippi River as possible.

By the end of our time together she had expressed her anger about dying and her rage over losing her husband so soon. She really missed Hank, and she wished she could see him again. I told her I hoped that somehow, some way, she could see him again. We talked about the fear under her anger: the fear that her pain would go untreated. We then talked about the sadness of dying. As we talked, her anger subsided, replaced by the forgotten memories of a wonderful life and the realization that a lot of people cared about her.

She understood not only that her anger was justified, but also that the unfortunate expression of her anger drove away the people she needed most.

I told the hospital staff what had happened. They had seen Beverly as "a pain" rather than as a woman in pain. I was able to convince them that her anger had not been directed at them and that if they treated her as a woman in pain, she would no longer be "a pain."

With Beverly's anger and fear dissipating, her loneliness faded. The next time the family called, she made a real effort to let them know that she was glad to hear from them and invited them down. Beverly shared with me that they were coming to visit her that afternoon, saying that she was looking forward to seeing them. The next day I stopped by to see how her visit had gone. Beverly was excited. She said to me, "I saw him," she laughed. "I saw Hank. My granddaughter has the same smile as he did. When she laughed, I saw him in her smile."

6

SPIRITUALITY AND DEATH

The right to seek spirituality.
The right to express feelings and emotions about death
  in one's own way.

The quest for spirituality is a search for a place of peace and safety. Many people begin looking for this place during the final chapters of their lives. They may do so through religion, on their own, or both. Whatever approach one chooses, it should be honored and supported, even if you think it is "incorrect." This last exploration is a rite of passage for the soul. It is also a right of the dying to be honored.

Ronald and Shirley had been married for forty-five years. Now both in their mid-sixties, they had spent most of their lives together. When I visited them shortly after Ronald's retirement, they talked about spending more time going to church, taking trips, planting a vegetable garden in the back-yard, and getting into shape. But things began to go wrong with their happy retirement plans almost immediately. Only a little exercise or activity left Ronald breathless and tired, so he went to the doctor for a checkup—his first in twenty years.

Unfortunately, the news was bad. Ronald had coronary artery disease and would have to undergo triple bypass surgery within the next few weeks. Shirley told me that although she was frightened by the prospect of surgery and terrified that her beloved husband might die, there was a "little gift" in the bad news. "It's made me realize more than ever that our time is limited," she explained as we sat together in the waiting room during the surgery. "It's gotten us to look back on life, talk about some things we never talked about before, and forgive each other for things we did. We've been able to forgive ourselves, accept life just as it is, and be grateful for all that has happened. Ron said that he realized that his life could end anytime and he wanted to get rid of all the grudges he was carrying. He wanted to forgive people."

"I didn't know Ronald was religious," I said.

"He wanted to get his house in order. He wanted to enjoy life and be at peace inside," she replied.

Fortunately, Ronald sailed through the bypass without any problems. He was soon up and around, more energetic than ever. The couple bought a dog and took long walks; they planted their garden and did volunteer work through their church. They traveled to Yosemite and Yellowstone and other parks, enjoying nature and life. And they continued to seek spirituality through their religion. "Not in a silly way," Shirley said. "But in the sense that we wanted to get rid of our anger and resentment."

Several years passed. Life was good for Ronald and Shirley. I called them one evening to make plans to get together over the upcoming weekend. Ronald said that they were eating dinner and he would call back soon. Fifteen or twenty minutes later he got up from the table and asked Shirley if he could get her anything. She smiled and said, "No thanks, I'm fine." He walked into the kitchen, set down a dish, and had a massive heart attack. He died instantly.

Shirley went into the kitchen a minute or two later. "I knew when I opened the door and saw him on the floor that he was dead. I called 911, then I lay down on the floor next to him. I felt his soul in my heart. I felt that he was okay and at peace. I lay there with tears coming out of my eyes, telling him how excited I felt when we first met. I caressed his face and said how grateful I was to have met him. Even now, when I think of Ronald dying in the kitchen, it comforts me to know that he'd examined his life and found peace, for the most part. And that's where he died, in peace."

Others have found comfort by following less traditional paths. Walter and Marion had been married for thirty-seven years. He was a novelist, she was an accountant; together they raised three boys in a small community outside of Santa Cruz, California. They lived in the same house for thirty years, and Marion worked at the same accounting firm in San Jose for fifteen years. Walter worked at home.

One day, after coughing up blood, Walter went to the doctor. The diagnosis was quickly made: He had a tumor in his lung. The surgery was performed a week later. It went well, and the doctor felt that all the cancerous tissue had been removed. However, Walter knew that a recurrence was always possible.

For the first time in his life, Walter wasn't sure what to do. He wasn't even sure that there was anything to do: He already ate a healthful diet, and he jogged along the beach every evening. But he didn't want to simply wait for the cancer to come back.

A friend of his, the editor of several of his books, suggested that he consult with a woman who did spiritual counseling. This took Walter by surprise. "A spiritual counselor?" he asked. "What does she do? Is she a psychologist, a social worker, a minister? Does she look into crystal balls? Do I have to burn incense and talk to spirits?"

"It's nothing like that," the editor replied. "She has no degrees, she's nondenominational. She just counsels from a spiritual viewpoint."

Curious, Walter made an appointment with the spiritual counselor. They discussed his condition, and he told her about his life. She asked him questions he had not thought about: Do you know why you are here? Do you know what you would like to do in your remaining time, however long that may be? What do you want to leave behind? "You've spent your entire life looking outside of yourself," she explained. "Now it's time to look inward."

All this struck a chord in Walter, who asked her for a list of books to read and questions to consider. He asked her to show him how to meditate.

As the weeks passed, Walter became more involved in his daily meditations and spiritual readings. He turned the two hours he used to devote every morning to reading the latest newspapers and magazines and the hour he had spent watching the news every night over to meditation and spiritual readings.

Marion, however, became increasingly upset. Finally she said: "Walter, this is not you. You don't read the papers, you don't watch the news. You're changing your life. It's like you're withdrawing from your old way of life. Don't you have enough to worry about without getting into all this spiritual stuff, thinking about the bogeyman? You have a serious disease, so we don't have time for this hocus-pocus."

"Why don't you try some of it with me?" Walter asked.

Marion was disdainful. "I only believe in what I can see and touch."

Despite his wife's strong objections, Walter continued to explore spirituality. In time, it became a way of life for him. Outwardly, his life remained pretty much the same. Inwardly, he let go of some of the financial and status concerns that had occupied his mind for much of his life. Overall, he felt much calmer and accepting. When he shared this with Marion, she said: "Good. Now that you got where you're going, you can stop with the counselor, stop with the books, stop with the meditation, stop with all this strange stuff. I want you to go back to the way you were. I'm worried about what our friends and family will think."

"This is my life now," he replied. "It helps me cope with what's going on. I don't mean for it to be threatening. It doesn't contradict our religion. I don't want to leave you out of it. I would like you to join me in any part of it you like. And I don't care what our friends think. I'm on a different playing field now, what matters is how I feel. I hope this can be a way for us to become closer, not separate us."

As time passed, Marion had many more discussions with Walter and their sons about his growing spirituality. The sons immediately understood what their father was doing. Eventually, Marion began to see that it was helping her husband. A year later she shared with me, "I'm glad he has it now. At first I thought it would be a one-time thing, which was okay. But it upset me that he stayed with it, because the cancer had already changed our lives and I didn't want any more changes. But Walter is a happier, more peaceful man, and that's all that matters to me."

Like Walter, many people facing life-threatening illnesses often examine their lives as they prepare to move from a place of body and spirit to the realm of spirit alone. They set aside the concerns of money, status, beauty, and possessions that have beset them during their lifetimes. Perhaps it's more correct to say that these things simply do not matter anymore as they reach out to grasp love, forgiveness, and peace.

We spend most of our lives looking outward until time, illness, and age force us to turn inward. We begin to examine our true natures, our souls, our spirits. Seeking spirituality as life draws to a close, reviewing life and asking questions about what comes next, is not a new concept. Human beings have probably been doing this since they became aware that everyone dies. Primal questions arise as we feel our time drawing to a close: Where do I go from here? Have I accomplished all that I was supposed to? Am I still whole and intact, despite my disease-ravaged body? Will I continue in one form or another? How do I find peace, the only thing that really matters now? Who am I really? Am I more than just a physical body? Do I have a spirit that will live on?

I believe so. In his book *Your Sacred Self,* Dr. Wayne Dyer says, "we are not human beings having a spiritual experience, we are spiritual beings having a human experience." Spirit is that part of you that will last forever, the unique thing that *is* you and will continue to live on after your body has ceased to function. When you look at someone who has just died, you can instantly tell that whatever it is that gives us the energy of life has left that body. That energy, that life force is the spirit or the soul. For some, spirit is the essence of who we are, for others it is God, and as their lifetimes draw to a close, people begin to explore the spirit that lasts forever.

Birth is not a beginning, it is merely a continuation, and death is not an ending, it is also a continuation. Your body came and your body will go, merely the suit of clothes you wear in this lifetime, but spirit is indestructible, for it is energy. As Einstein pointed out, energy can neither be created nor destroyed: It was, it is, and it always will be.

The word "spirituality" means different things to different people. For some, it is the recognition of a higher power or their deeper selves. For many, it means getting in touch with God. For others, spirituality is simply the act of loving. It is not *what* we love, such as flowers or ice cream, but the *act* of loving, the feeling of loving. Being spiritual means trying to react to the everyday challenges of life in a loving and peaceful way. It is easy to be spiritual sitting on a mountaintop where no one can insult you, steal your money, or cut you off in traffic. Finding peace in a world where people die, crime goes unpunished, co-workers annoy you, and goals seem out of reach is a different matter.

THE FIVE STAGES OF SPIRITUAL RECONCILIATION

Our belief systems shape our lives. We believe that if we are educated, we will get a good job. If we accumulate money, we will be safe from hunger. If we eat right and exercise often, we will be healthy. We believe that pills will work, that medical technology will keep disease at bay, and that doctors will save us. Inevitably, our beliefs fade as we realize that we will not live forever, no matter how smart, rich, or healthy we may be, no matter how good our doctors are. As the end approaches, we realize that we must leave behind families, friends, money, possessions, status, technology, and society itself. At that point it is natural to feel the desire to believe that there is rhyme and reason to the world, that everything happens for the best, and that our lives have had meaning. As we must let go of everything we have known, faith allows us to escape the fear that all is random and meaningless.

We find our comfort and faith in the love and peace that is spirituality. It gives meaning and order to life, especially as one is leaving this life. Neither philosophy nor technology can give us these precious gifts. When all else must leave us, spirituality and faith remain.

Elisabeth Kübler-Ross has described the five steps we go through as we face death: denial, anger, bargaining, depression, and acceptance. There is a similar approach to spirituality. Upon developing a genuine desire to explore their spiritual selves, people go through five stages of spiritual reconciliation: expression, responsibility, forgiveness, acceptance, and gratitude.

Expression—Many people have trouble accepting the demise of their physical selves because they're blocked by anger. Being human, we all make judgments, we all hate, we all blame others, we all become furious, and we all behave in petty ways. Sometimes we're justified in doing so; more often we're not. As far as healing is concerned, it doesn't matter. For healing to take place, we must overcome our taboos and express our feelings. You've been taught not to say that you're jealous of your sister because you think your mother loved her more than you. You shudder to say that you hate your father for the way he treated you.

We fear that we will be punished if we express our "ugly" feelings but in fact the opposite is true. We are rewarded for releasing our anger by making ourselves ready for peace. You don't have to tell your father or sister that you hate them. You can say it to a trusted friend, you can whisper it into the air, or you can scream it into your pillow. Once you do, the angry thoughts begin to dissipate. The hate that held you hostage disappears. You can also tell God why you're upset, if that's the case. Anger toward God is a problem for many. I've worked with people from various faiths, and I've found that they often need permission to become angry with God. How could He have allowed Mom to suffer so horribly and die so young? How could He have allowed Dad to be cheated out of his life savings? How can He now allow me to suffer so much, then die, leaving behind a widow and three young children? How can He be so cruel and callous? Many of us feel that it's absolutely taboo to admit to being angry with God, but until we admit to our feelings, we cannot heal. I've had people express their anger verbally, I've even had them express their anger by hitting the bed with a baseball bat. God understands that you need to express and release your feelings in order to love.

We may also be blocked by our negative feelings toward our diseases. In her book *A Return to Love,* Marianne Williamson describes the technique of writing your disease a letter and many people I work with say it's a powerful technique. Exercises like this help us admit to and confront our buried feelings. They also help us get in touch with our deeper, spiritual selves. People I have cared for have written "Dear Cancer" letters, "Dear Leukemia" letters, and "Dear AIDS" letters. In these letters, they talk about their anger at their diseases, they share their feelings about what has happened. Some ask their diseases to leave, others ask that they live together in harmony.

Responsibility—People have often said that facing a life-challenging illness has improved the quality of their lives. Specifically, it helped them take responsibility for their actions, thoughts, and lives. They know that they're not to blame for their diseases and that dying does not mean that they have somehow failed. They also understand that they have played a role in all that has happened to them in life.

Harvey, suddenly faced with pancreatic cancer and given only a short time to live, gained a new understanding of responsibility.

"I used to blame everyone else for my problems," he said. "I'd say that my ex-wife ruined our marriage, my lousy business partner was only out for himself, my friends betrayed me. But now I look back on all the bad things that ever happened to me and realize that they all had one common denominator: me! I was involved in all of them. Sure, my wife quit trying to make our marriage work and my partner was a selfish crook and my friends didn't always see things my way, but I chose them. And you know what? It's not just *their* fault. I made mistakes in the marriage; I wasn't the best business partner or friend. *I* have to take responsibility for my life. I don't want to live as a victim, and I certainly don't want to die as one."

Harvey learned that he is not to blame for the misdeeds of others, but that he bears responsibility for all that has happened to *him*.

Forgiveness—In the end, our diseases stop spreading, our hearts no longer beat, and our minds cease thinking. So do our fights, grudges, and judgments end. Whether we like it or not, our part of the quarrel will be over, for we will no longer be here. The dying understand this intuitively, which is why they often have a meeting with forgiveness. To forgive does not mean to accept bad behavior. When we forgive, we release ourselves from the binds of hates and hurts. When I forgive you for cheating on me fifteen years ago, I'm not saying that it's all right to hurt people. I am saying, however, that I understand that you made a mistake, I've made mistakes, and we all make mistakes. I'm no longer going to define you or our entire relationship by that one mistake.

Unforgiveness is an open wound. We forgive ourselves and others because we want to die whole. I am constantly struck by how strong a role forgiveness plays. I have seen two sisters who have not spoken for thirty years become best friends again as one of them is faced with death, because they finally forgive one another for something that happened three decades ago. I have seen a mother, a father, and their son come back into one another's lives after the parents had disowned the son for marrying outside his religion. It was not until his father became ill that they realized their time together was limited and that forgiveness was the only thing that could lead to a reconciliation. I am touched by the story of a Hindu man whose son was murdered by Muslims during the religious wars that convulsed India as the nation prepared to become independent from Great Britain in the 1940s. The grieving Hindu man went to see Mahatma Gandhi, who was also a Hindu, asking, "How can I possibly forgive the Muslims? How can I ever find peace again with so much hate in my heart for those who have killed my only son?" Gandhi suggested that the man adopt an orphaned Muslim boy and raise him as his own.

We're afraid that forgiving the people who have hurt us is the same as absolving them of their misdeeds. But we forgive for our own sake, when we realize that holding on to grudges forces us to live in unhappiness. When people are reluctant to forgive, I tell them, maybe it's not up to us to punish. Meanwhile, this is your death. Do you want to die awash in hatred? Our final acts are the ones that will be remembered by our loved ones. Few of us would choose hatred and revenge as our exit lines. We'd prefer to be remembered for kindness and joy.

Forgiving ourselves is just as much a part of spiritual growth as forgiving others. Most people are very hard on themselves at the end, remembering all the things they've done wrong, whether little or large, and wondering if they can ever be forgiven. I tell them that if they feel that they cannot forgive themselves, they should simply ask their God or Higher Power for help. We can die in unforgiveness; that's an option and some people do die that way. But many choose to make way for inner peace by forgiving.

Acceptance—I remember very well the stout forty-two-year-old banker who grasped his dying father's shoulders as the older man lay in his hospital bed and practically shouted at him: "Dad! Fight it! Fight it! You've been a fighter all your life, you can beat this!" And I remember so many other loved ones sobbing, "How could he die so young?" and "She was such a good person, it's unfair that she should have to die."

We live in a fix-it society with the technology to repair many broken things at our fingertips. We forget that we've all been deliberately designed to "end" one day. When that ending happens, there's nothing to fix. Optimism and a fighting spirit are good things, but at a certain point optimism becomes denial. It's important that patients be willing to fight when fighting is appropriate, but we will all face that moment in life when it is time to stop fighting, to stop treating death as the enemy. This is not giving up. It's accepting what is happening, riding the horse in the direction it's going. Once the final death process has started it cannot be stopped, any more than a woman in labor can be prevented from delivering her child.

We don't have to like what we accept. We think that to accept something is to somehow make it good or desirable. However, I think we can own our feelings, and accept what is happening. I believe individuals on their deathbed can honestly say: "I don't want to die," yet accept that they are dying.

Accepting that life is complete is perhaps the most difficult of the steps toward spirituality. We find it especially hard to accept death when it's "premature." People will say "he was so young" or "she never got to retire" or "there were so many things that he never got to do," as if those lives had been incomplete. From our vantage point, it often seems so. It's hard for us to accept that a five-year-old who dies from leukemia or a thirty-year-old felled by breast cancer has had a complete life. It's only when the deceased is eighty or ninety years old that we allow ourselves the peaceful feeling that they had a complete life.

Every life is complete. The only two requirements for a life to be complete are birth and death. People may say that life isn't complete without a family, or a career, or a certain number of years, but whether we like it or not, birth and death define a life. An eighteen-year-old with cystic fibrosis married a seventeen-year-old who also had the disease. Before she died a year later, she felt that she had had a complete life. A twelve-year-old boy with cancer said he wouldn't miss old age; he'd never planned on it. A forty-four-year-old man with AIDS said: "Many people with this disease die in their twenties. I accept that I've had many years of life." There may be things we wish had happened—more time, more opportunities, and more experiences. But their absence doesn't mean that a life was incomplete.

Gratitude—Having expressed one's feelings, taken responsibility for all that has occurred, forgiven oneself and others, and accepted what is now occurring, the person on a spiritual journey becomes profoundly grateful for his or her life, for both the good times and the bad.

Grateful for the bad times? Yes. Many women who were dumped by philandering husbands are grateful for the good times they had, for the children they produced together. A woman who had been cheated out of ten thousand dollars early in her business career was grateful, "for I learned a good lesson early on that only cost me ten thousand dollars, while most of my friends didn't learn it until much later and were hit a lot harder." Forty-two-year-old Mark, who lost his eyesight in an accident at age fifteen and was now dying of lymphoma, told me he remembered the colors. His favorite was blue. "Some are born blind. They have never seen blue. I am so thankful; I can still see it in my mind." And Eric's mother, who knew that she would soon bury her thirty-two-year-old son, his body shriveled and ravaged by AIDS, prayed to God, thanking Him for giving her such a beautiful boy and thirty-two years together.

Expression, responsibility, forgiveness, acceptance, and gratitude, all leading to reconciliation: These are the steps I've seen countless people take on the road to spirituality. And the peace they attain is medicine for their souls.

THE GIFT OF SPIRITUALITY

Healthy people are usually astonished when someone with AIDS, cancer, or another terrible disease says that they have been given a gift. Diseases are not gifts, but they bring with them unexpected benefits. All of our experiences open our hearts wider or close them a little. When we're faced with life-threatening diseases we look back on our lives, sweeping the negative thoughts aside to make room for love, forgiveness, gratitude, and peace.

Spirituality is the gift, a gift no one has ever offered to return. Over the years, people of all ages and backgrounds, faced with life-threatening illnesses, have shared these gifts with me:

- *"Now that my life is threatened I realize that life itself has been a gift. Not something owed to me, but a true gift."*

- *"I'm less afraid of life because I have found peace in death. Life is now an adventure to be savored until I die."*

- *"I realize that life is to be lived. It does not need to be taken so seriously."*

- *"I've found a new, more authentic identity for myself. It's based on who I am, not what I did. I am a human being, not a human doing."*

- *"I am not defined by my achievements or failures. All those great and terrible moments of life were just that—moments. They were not me, they do not define me."*

- *"I live in the here and now. I'm no longer counting on the future, or hiding from it."*

- *"I've let go of my negative feelings, finding love and happiness here and now."*

- *"I realize that I am truly a unique person. No one has ever seen or experienced the world quite the way I have, and no one ever will. In one million years, there will never be another me."*

- *"Now that I know what is really important, I find more love in my relationships. We talk about what is real and important to us. We share ourselves more. I've become closer with those I love."*

- *"I have found purpose in life. I make decisions on what I want to do with the time I have left. I do what gives my life meaning and makes my heart sing. I paint, write, volunteer, act, and parent."*

- *"I am no longer a victim of life."*

- *"I have forgiven myself and others. I feel better about myself, and have more loving relationships."*

- *"I have found peace."*

Many people have received gifts like these when they faced life-challenging illnesses. Those who went into remission tell me that they realized the gifts weren't just for the dying—they were also for the living. The great playwright George Bernard Shaw showed that the living can glory in spirituality when he wrote:

> *This is the true joy in life: The being used for a purpose recognized by yourself as a mighty one. The being a force of nature, instead of a feverish, selfish little clod of ailments and grievances complaining that the world will not devote itself to making you happy. I am of the opinion that my life belongs to the whole community, and as long as I live, it is my privilege to do for it whatever I can.*
>
> *I want to be thoroughly used up when I die—for the harder I work, the more I live. I rejoice in life for its own sake. Life is no "brief candle" to me; it is a sort of splendid torch which I have got hold of for the moment, and I want to make it burn as brightly as possible before handing it on to future generations.*

In 1973, when my mother lay in a coma in a New Orleans hospital, my older cousin Sylvia, a nurse, flew in from Boston. Sylvia, my father, and I sat in the hospital lobby, waiting to see my mother for the ten minutes we were allowed every two hours. Sylvia stayed with us for a few days, spending as much time as possible with my mother.

Years later I said to Sylvia: "You were a nurse. Did you know she was dying?"

"Of course, that was very clear," she answered.

"Why didn't you tell us?"

"You didn't ask. And when I tried to approach the topic, I

got clear signals that you were not ready to face it. So I didn't think it was my place to force the topic on you."

She was right, of course. It's not our place to tell anyone, before they are ready to hear it, that his or her loved one is dying, or to insist on having a conversation about dying. You can give people only the information that they're ready to receive, and that depends upon their level of spirituality and understanding.

We each find spirituality in our own way and at our own pace. Accepting things as they are also means accepting another's pace in the discovery of spirituality. You may find their pace either too fast or too slow, but it's important that you do not interfere in the process. Cousin Sylvia knew that my father and I were handling as much as we could and wisely decided not to interfere. She understood that when we were ready to know the realities of my mother's condition, we would ask. As the old saying goes, when you're ready to know something, someone will show up and tell you what you need to know.

Every dying person has the right to seek spirituality, in his own way, in his own time. They also have the right *not* to seek spirituality. Seeking or not seeking spirituality is a private matter.

THE LIMITS OF SPIRITUALITY

Robert, whom you remember from Chapter 2, called me recently to say, "They found another lump. I have to start chemotherapy right away and probably have to undergo surgery. I thought I was cured. What spiritual lesson didn't I learn last time?"

Some people believe that if they become spiritual enough, they will be able to cure their diseases. That, however, would be magic, not spirituality! Spirituality is not a cure for disease. It's our reconnection with ourselves, with others, and with life, even in the face of death. It is our seeking of peace. As far as lessons are concerned, maybe Robert's lesson was to accept things just as they are. Maybe he hadn't done anything wrong at all. Maybe things were unfolding just as they were intended.

Finding inner peace, forgiving yourself and others, and being calmer do have beneficial effects on the body, but spirituality by itself is not a cure, and falling ill does not mean that you are doing something wrong. True spirituality is not about blaming or finding fault. It's about reaching into the purest part of yourself, the part that is connected to love, the part that is (if you believe it to be) connected to God, the part that is beyond the body and health or disease. Spirituality is concerned with the mind and spirit, not the body.

A SPIRITUAL PASSING

Spirituality holds a special fascination for the dying and has eased the transition for many. But it's not always easy to face death with peace and serenity. This letter shows how difficult, yet ultimately rewarding, the path can be. It was written as an open letter by a man named Bill.

Dear Friends:

Six or seven months ago I lay in a hospital bed convinced that I was going to die. AIDS, cancer and pneumonia all seemed to be fighting to claim my life. At that time, I felt very terrified that I might die and go to hell, or just not go on at all. But my time had not come. The time since then has been a precious gift, in which great healing has occurred. After months of medical treatment, followed by months of holistic treatment and months of spiritual work on myself, I am free.

My partner's remarkable support, a spiritual guide, a meditation partner, several meditation retreats, support from wonderful friends, and a lot of work within my own heart has left me at peace.

For many months, my idea of healing was that of curing my body. I gave it my best try and I am proud of this fact. I was even given several months of relative health and energy. At that time, I often expressed my certainty that I could heal my body with my own healing powers. I still believe these healing powers exist, but as my physical health reached a point where optimism about my health would have had to become self-denial, I realized the need to accept my own impending death and physical mortality. I also realized that self-compassion meant feeling in my heart that even death was not a sign of weakness or failure. This seems to be the ultimate act of self-acceptance. I thank God for it.

All this did not come easily. I have wept many times. I have gotten angry and confused. But I have learned that the only way out of the pain is through the pain. A hard lesson to learn . . .

In the past six months I have started my own production company, which produced a calendar of my own photography. I have worked within this community to heighten awareness of the disease. I have grown closer than ever to my family, my partner and my friends. I am very proud and thankful for these things. Most important, I have come to accept myself exactly as I am. This is the greatest gift of all.

And so my healing has occurred. Soon my body will be dropping away from me, like a cocoon, and my spirit will fly like a butterfly—beautiful and perfect. I don't claim to know where exactly it is that I am going, but my heart tells me it is filled with light and love.

An open heart is an infinitely greater blessing than death is a tragedy. Let us all take comfort in this knowledge.

Love,
Bill

I believe Bill died a few days after writing this letter. He had faced his fears, found peace, and moved on.

7

CHILDREN AND DEATH

The right of children to participate in death.
The right to understand the process of death.
The right not to die alone.

Our children watch us, they model us, they impersonate us. We are always teaching them. When we are affectionate, we teach them love. When we are amused, we teach them humor. When we are afraid, we teach them fear. But we believe that seeing, talking, or thinking about death will harm our children so we "protect" them from it. We shoo them out of the room when Aunt Betsy is lying ill in bed, about to die. We don't tell them why Aunt Betsy has suddenly vanished. If we do, we use euphemisms, saying that Aunt Betsy has "gone to sleep" or to a "better place."

When I counsel patients with terminal illnesses and their families, the subject of education for children about death occasionally comes up. Most were not prepared at all when death visited their family. Franklin, a fifty-six-year-old electrician who has diabetes, had a typical first exposure to death: "They said that my grandmother had 'gone to sleep,' but no one would tell me when she was going to wake up. Then they left me in the car at her funeral. I was only five but I remember every detail perfectly. I was nine when my mother died of tuberculosis. God, I wanted so much to see her, to say good-bye to her, but they wouldn't let me. Everyone else filed past the casket to say good-bye except me. 'It's better for you,' they told me. 'You'll understand later.' Yeah, well, all I understood is that death was a horrible thing and I never got to say good-bye to my grandmother or mother. How did they expect me to learn that death is a normal part of life if they kept hiding it from me? I don't blame them. They did what they thought was right. But maybe if they hadn't treated death like such a horrible thing I wouldn't be terrified of it. I can't even go to the cemetery to visit my mother's or grandmother's graves. Anything to do with death or dying or being dead paralyzes me. I want my daughter to have a better view of death."

We do not teach our children that for every spring there will be a summer, then a fall and a winter. We do not help them understand that what lives also dies. Children who do not learn that every spring *must* eventually give way to a winter and that every life *must* produce a death have difficulty coping with loss. There's no cruelty in allowing children to learn that their loved ones, their pets, and eventually they themselves will die. On the contrary, it's a gift of love.

We only fool ourselves when we believe that we can shield our children from death or that they are unaware of it. As with many of my generation, one of my earliest memories of death is seeing the movie *Bambi* and watching as he mourned his mother, shot by the hunter. Death plays a large role in every young life. When a child cries for its mother in the next room, he is grieving the separation. One of the first games we learn to play is "peek-a-boo." Someone you love is there, then all of a sudden she's gone. Psychologists tell us that young children really believe their play partners have vanished, at least temporarily.

Ring-around-a-rosy is actually a death-poem British children began chanting when the Great Plague left dead bodies lying in the streets. "Rosy" refers to parts of the body reddened by the disease, "posies" to the flowers people frantically stuffed into their pockets for protection against the plague. But when children began chanting this poem centuries ago the people who "all fall down" didn't get back up again. Meanwhile, children play other games that involve death, they watch television shows, movies, and video games in which death is common. Is this the only input we want them to have?

PREPARING CHILDREN FOR DEATH

"I had no concept of death," Diane told me. "I was five years old when my mother died in a car accident. She went out one day very healthy, the next thing I hear is that she's never coming back again because she's gone to a better place. I wanted to be with her in this better place, and I heard my aunts talking about a car accident. So I pushed my bike to the top of the hill we lived on, got on, and pedaled as fast as I could down, trying to crash into the wall at the house at the bottom of the hill. I really thought this 'death' thing, whatever it was, was caused by accidents and it let you go to this better place where Mommy was. Luckily, I fell off my bike onto a soft lawn so I only twisted my ankle."

Children hear about death whether we like it or not. It's best to explain death to our children *before* someone they love is dying, before the situation is emotionally charged. This "facts of life" talk needn't be formal, with charts and slides.

You can simply introduce them to the concept by pointing to dying leaves that have fallen from trees, to wilted flowers. They'll quickly understand that green leaves turn yellow then brown, that brightly colored flowers grow, bloom, and die. If you and your child happen upon a dead bird in the woods, you can explain that the bird had a life, but that everything eventually dies. The bird's time on earth is over. The bird will be missed by its family, but that's the way of life. Everything has its season, every spring turns to summer, to fall, and finally to winter.

You can teach your child about funerals and rituals when a fish in the aquarium dies. If your child wants to bury the fish in the backyard, help him. Show him how it's done, let him see that we continue to respect bodies even after the soul has flown. If you send the child away, then quickly flush the fish down the toilet, you are teaching the child that beloved things simply disappear. But if you use the fish's passing as an opportunity to discuss death, to place it in perspective and give the child an opportunity to grieve, you teach him how to grieve and to understand that death is always a part of life.

It also helps to explain illness to children. If Aunt Betsy has cancer, explain that Aunt Betsy's cancer is a very serious illness. Depending on the child's level of understanding, you can stop there or go on to explain, for example, that Aunt Betsy is no longer like the green leaf on the tree branch. Now that she's ill, she's more like the yellow leaf that clings to the branch. The doctor is trying to make her strong, healthy, and "green," but there's a chance she'll become "brown" and will let go of the branch.

Take time to explain how diseases can affect people differently. It's vital to distinguish between major and minor illness, lest children be afraid that they will die the next time they get a cold, or that Mommy's flu will be the death of her. Explain that although Uncle Horace died of cancer, Grandfather recovered from his cancer and is doing quite well. This will help quell fear of cancer and other diseases by letting them know, early on, that there's always hope for recovery.

Having these talks with our children can be difficult. They may bring up painful memories we'd prefer not to face. We fear that we'll scare our children unnecessarily. We're afraid they will ask us questions we cannot answer. It's perfectly fine to say "I don't know." If you believe that people go to heaven when they die, say so. If you believe that we don't know what happens, say so. Be honest and open when speaking about death, *especially* when you don't know the answer to a question.

WHEN DEATH OCCURS

Children are understandably puzzled and frightened when death happens in the family. When a death occurs, children need to be reassured that they are loved, that they will be cared for, and that the dying person will be in the child's heart and memories forever. We also need to reassure them that everyone will not die at once. They may fear that since Uncle John died last year and Aunt Betsy is dying now, their parents will pass away soon. We may need to explain that Aunt Betsy is old, but the rest of us are young and will probably live for a long time. We also need to assure them that life will continue. We loved Aunt Betsy and will miss her greatly, but life will go on pretty much as it was before she got sick. We'll have breakfast, lunch, and dinner as always, we'll return to work and school soon, we'll go to the park and visit friends, just as we did before. Aunt Betsy's death saddens us but will not completely change our daily lives.

It's also important to let our children know what is happening when a loved one becomes ill, in an age-appropriate manner that they can understand. If the child's grandmother is gravely ill, you can point out that life will be different for a while, that you will be spending more time at the hospital and that the usual family vacation in the mountains will be canceled this year. If they want to know why you aren't spending time with them, you can say, "I don't believe that I have much time left with your grandmother. It seems unfair now, but I want to spend more time with her while I can. You and I will have a lifetime together."

When you speak of illness, death, or dying to your children, be honest, simple, and brief. Wait for their reaction before going on. If they're satisfied with what you've said, fine. If not, if they seem disturbed or ask questions, offer more information. If you tell your son Mark that "Your father is sick, it's serious, and we're worried about him," stop and look at Mark's reaction before going on. If Mark says, "Okay," then runs out to play, that's all the information he needs or wants right now. But if he asks, "Is Daddy going to die?" or "How did he get sick?" he's ready to learn more. Don't bombard children with information they haven't asked for and can't understand, and don't withhold anything if they are ready to hear it. Tell them a little, then watch for their reaction. They'll let you know if they need more.

Children will often become jealous of the dying, who seem to be getting all the attention, especially if it's a sibling who is ill. They often move from jealousy to guilt if the ill person dies. Sometimes we unknowingly make them feel terribly guilty, shouting, "How can you even think of going to the movies when your sister is so sick?" Going to the movies may be the last thing on your mind, but a child is supposed to think about going to the movies and playing soccer and vacationing in the mountains. Children haven't yet learned about the relative importance of movies versus death. This is a chance to teach them. Explain the dilemma. Explain that you too are having a hard time and would prefer to be at the movies but that Sis *is* sick. Explain that hard choices have to be made.

Be careful about unknowingly idealizing the dying. The relatives gathered in the living room may speak about how wonderful poor, dying Debbie is, but younger brother Mark knows that she liked to tie his hair in knots and steal his comic books. He knows she's far from perfect but may feel that he has to live up to the ridiculously high standard the relatives have set for him by idolizing Debbie. There's a great temptation to see only perfection, especially when children are dying, but it's better for everyone to keep in mind that the dying are human.

WHAT CHILDREN MAY THINK

If we don't tell our children the truth, what they imagine will always be worse. Most of us don't realize the powerful implications of our white lies and euphemisms:

- *If we simply tell them that sister Debbie has gone to sleep, they may become afraid to go to bed.*
- *If we simply tell them that God has taken Aunt Betsy away, they may believe that a cruel God snatches good people away.*

❧ *If we simply tell them that death is darkness and nothingness, they may become afraid of the dark.*

❧ *If we simply tell them that they were so good that God wanted them with Him, they may fear to be good.*

❧ *If we simply tell them that Daddy is going on a really long trip, they may believe that Daddy has abandoned them.*

If we give them double messages we risk leaving them more frightened and puzzled than ever. If we say that Daddy has gone to heaven where everything is beautiful and we're so happy that he's there, but we're sobbing as we say it, they'll sense that something is wrong. Why is Mommy crying if Daddy's in a wonderful place? It makes much more sense to a child if we say "Daddy has gone to heaven. It's really a wonderful place, but I miss him very much. I'm glad he got to go to heaven, but I wish he could have stayed with us. And he wishes that he could have stayed with us longer."

Children learn by watching and doing. If we shoo them out of Mommy's bedroom while Mommy is dying, they learn that death is a terrible and mysterious thing. Suppose we allow them to participate as much as they can, given their age and emotional states. We can bring a young child into Mommy's bedroom and say, "Let's massage Mommy's feet now," or "Fill up her water glass," or even just "Give Mommy a hug." Doing this won't make them like death, but it will help them to accept it, to realize that they can be a part of their loved one's life right up to the end. They'll have learned how to care, how to help, how to love, and how to deal with death, even if only a little.

Aileen Getty, of the J. Paul Getty oil family, has known

since 1985 that she's infected with the HIV virus. Aileen, who is Elizabeth Taylor's former daughter-in-law, has sons, one eleven and one twelve years old. I asked Aileen whether children should be allowed to "participate" in the death of a loved one. "I've been through this with my kids," she said. "If I fall down, they pick me up. They change my tubes. My kids have slept in my bed, tubes and all. They're proud that I'm their mother. I'm trying to help them resolve the process as it happens, as opposed to them trying to resolve a memory many years from now. I didn't have the opportunity to resolve anything with my mother when she died. I had to go on, become an adult and deal with it as best as I could. My children know about my disease and what might happen to me. I tell them because the less we know the more we imagine, the more we create. And what we create is more terrible than reality."

A forty-nine-year-old advertising executive dying of malignant melanoma had his ten-year-old son help him pack up his office as the disease forced him to retire. "I thought by doing this it would help my son put work into a proper perspective in his life, as well as open the conversation for us to talk about what work has meant to me during my life, what life has meant to me, as well as talking about dying. I've spent so much time teaching him how one begins life, I want to now teach him how to wind down life."

HELPING CHILDREN GRIEVE

Caught up in the natural narcissism of early life, children often believe they are responsible for unpleasant events. They may genuinely believe that Grandpa's terrible illness, the thing that has everyone sobbing and whispering, is their fault. They may think that Grandpa is sick because they were mad at him or because they didn't listen to him last time he visited. And what do you think happens when a harried mother repeatedly tells her children that "You'll be the death of me," and then she dies?

It's not only young children who find themselves wracked by guilt for "making" someone die. Janet, a hospice nurse herself, has been in therapy for most of her life because of something that happened when she was a teenager. While she and her father were having a fight over whether or not she should be allowed to take the car one night, she angrily said: "Drop dead, Dad!" Soon afterward, he dropped dead of a sudden heart attack. She never wanted him to die, she was simply using a phrase she had heard her father use when he was angry. Like him, she spoke without understanding the possible (or impossible) consequences of her words. And like other children and teenagers, she lacked the maturity to separate her angry thoughts from the unrelated fact of her father's death.

It's important for us to explain to children that Mommy's illness or Aunt Betsy's death is not their fault.

Four Steps to Help Children Grieve

While Colleen, who was suffering from end-stage kidney disease, was still able to get around, she took her twelve-year-old son and eight-year-old daughter to her father's grave. He had died a few years earlier. "I wanted to take them there," she explained, "to remind them of their grandfather and to let them see me crying. I wanted them to see someone grieving, and to understand what it was. How else will they learn?"

Children have to learn to grieve, just as they learn to ride a bicycle or play the piano. We are their models, and they learn to grieve and express their feelings by watching us. It's important to let our children see us grieve. It may be upsetting to them to see Mommy cry, but it's even more upsetting to be pushed out of the room when they know that Mommy is about to burst into tears.

We tend to teach children to bottle up their feelings, to "act like a man," or to "be a grown-up." Unfortunately, that's not a productive way to mourn; it does nothing but shove down feelings that will burst to the surface again. Here are four steps we can take to help our children mourn productively:

❧ Help them understand and make sense out of what has happened, or is happening. *Tell them the truth—that Aunt Betsy has died and will not be coming to visit anymore. Explain that Aunt Betsy had a serious disease, and tell them the name of the disease. Let them know that not all diseases are as serious as the one Aunt Betsy had, that everyone else is in good health, and that life will soon be back to normal. Say that Aunt Betsy is gone, but that we'll remember her and love her forever.*

❧ Help them grieve or express their emotional responses to the present or anticipated loss. *Children need validation. They need to know that their feelings are appropriate. Say something like: "I understand that you're angry because Grandpa died. It makes me angry, too. I know you were mad because we weren't able to do fun things this past year because I was taking care of Grandpa. I wanted to spend more time with you but I had to help Grandpa. I know you're sad that he's gone." Teach your children to cry by letting them see you crying. Let them know that it's okay to be angry. If they don't seem to be upset by the death, tell them that's okay, too. They don't have to pretend to feel upset if they weren't close to the person who died.*

❧ Teach them that life goes on. *Let them know that even though Mommy is enormously upset over Grandpa's death and would like never to go back to work, you're taking three days off to take care of yourself then returning to work. Let them know that they can also take time off to grieve, but then they have to return to school. We may be sad for a long time and we'll always miss Grandpa, but life goes on and Grandpa would want us to go on.*

❧ Help them commemorate the loss, whether formally or informally. *Light a candle together. Take time to tell stories. Say a prayer or put up a favorite picture. Shannon and her young son bring flowers to her late husband's grave on his birthday and Christmas. Vincent wrote a check, and his son donated his allowance, to Mothers Against Drunk Drivers in memory of the son's friend who died in a car accident. On the first birthday after Grandfather died, the Ellis family took out the old family albums. They looked through them, each selecting a favorite picture of Grandfather and talking about it. These small but important actions help to externalize the loss and encourage the expression of feelings.*

LETTING CHILDREN SAY GOOD-BYE

Many people feel that children should not be allowed at funerals, either because the children will be upset or they'll be distracting. When deciding whether or not your child should attend, treat a funeral just as you would a wedding, graduation, or any other formal event. If you're going to be busy at

the ceremony and can't attend to your child, then have someone else you and your child trust mind him or her. I've
found, however, that children generally behave quite well at
funerals if they're given three things:

- Prior preparation. *Tell them what's going to happen, where they'll
  be sitting, for how long, and that people may be crying. If the child
  wants to go, he should be allowed to. If the child says he doesn't
  want to go, his choice should be honored. If he's old enough to
  understand, explain that this will be a good chance to say good-bye
  to the deceased.*

- Support. *Make sure the child has someone to comfort her if she is
  upset or grieving. If you're going to be busy during the funeral, or if
  you're grieving too much to help your child, find someone who can
  help.*

- Follow-up after the funeral. *Talk about what has happened,
  what it meant and what they thought of it. Help your children put
  the loss and the ceremony in proper perspective.*

I was recently at Marty's funeral. Marty was an energetic eighty-year-old who lived by a lake and was a dedicated fisherman. He loved to teach his many young grandchildren how to fish, how to "read the water," and how to
"get into the fish's mind." I was amazed to see the grandchildren, who ranged from two to ten years old, rushing up
to his coffin as it was lowered into the ground. A few
adults, worried that the children wouldn't be able to grasp
what was happening, wanted to stop them. But their parents said that it was okay for the young ones to watch. As
the coffin was being lowered, a child who couldn't have
been more than five said to another, "Oh, wow! Grandpa's
being reeled in!" Children will often intertwine things that

happened in life with the rituals of death. This serves a useful purpose, helping to make the legacy of the person who died ongoing.

WHEN A PARENT IS DYING

If you're the one who is dying, if you will be leaving children behind, you are facing a parent's worse fear. Franklin, the electrician dying of complications of diabetes, told me that he had fervently prayed to God to keep him alive until his daughter had grown up. "I've protected her throughout her life, but what can I do for her when I'm gone?" he asked rhetorically.

Child specialist Kathleen McCue suggests that you do three things. Tell your child that you are seriously ill, name the disease you are struggling with, and tell them what you think will happen. Don't offer more information than is asked for, and let them ask questions at their own pace. If you feel that you will not get better, explain who will take care of them and how. Remind them that even though you will soon be gone, they will always have memories of you, that they'll never forget the times you had and the love you shared. Tell them that these times and the love will live forever.

Lois and her husband, Russ, told their nine-year-old son of his mother's breast cancer. They told him what cancer was and that it was serious. They explained that people sometimes die of cancer, but it looked as though this cancer would be surgically removed and Mother would be fine. They said that they did not think she would die of the cancer.

Some parents write letters or make videotapes for their children. Even though they've passed on, parents can remain a part of their children's lives. Franklin decided he wanted to continue on in his daughter's life in this more tangible way. Before being fully confined to bed, he made several videotapes of himself. The first for when she started dating, the second for when she began college, a third for when she was about to get married, a fourth for when she became a parent, and one more for when she just missed him.

In that one he says: "I know if you're watching this tape you're probably missing me. You may wonder if I miss you, too. I can tell you that I do. I want you to know that the hardest thing for me in dying was leaving you behind. I tried and tried and tried not to leave you, and in the end I had to go. I know you will think of me often, as I will of you. On those days when you're busy in your life at school or with friends, and out of the blue I pop into your mind for no reason, just know that at that moment I'm thinking of you. There will be times in your life when you may feel lonely, but you will never be alone. I will always be as close as your heart."

We hope that the words we leave our children will continue to comfort them, that they will be symbolic of how we lived and how we died. The teaching we do now will help shape our children's perception of loss, affecting many generations to come. We spend a great deal of time teaching our children about life. This is a profound opportunity to teach them how we care for loved ones in their last days, to help build their belief system around death and loss rather than leave them with a mystery, and to model for them how we honor the memory of our loved ones.

8

The Physiology of Death

The right to understand the process of death.
The right to have all questions answered honestly and
fully.

When people were discharged from the hospitals in the late 1970s so that they could die at home, doctors and nurses spent a great deal of time orienting and preparing their families, teaching them about medications, medical equipment, home safety, and other issues. If a member of the medical team asked, "When we meet the family, do we tell them what's going to happen when the patient dies?" someone would invariably reply, "They'll find out soon enough, on their own."

Death occurs, whether we know what is happening or not, but we have the right to know and understand what is happening, whether we ourselves are dying or we're caring for an ailing loved one.

Death is talked about, written about, illustrated in art and shown in movies, but the actual moment of death is rarely seen, even by the doctors who care for us and are called upon to pronounce us dead. Few of us have seen it more than once.

It's hard to describe the "usual" death, for every death, like every life, is unique. It does not follow an exact sequence of events. Some of the events described in this chapter may occur, some may not. While these events are signs of impending death, they may also occur in nonterminal conditions. There are few certainties where death is concerned.

When I began to do research for this chapter I asked a physician friend where I could find descriptions of what happens physically when we die. He had no idea. He said he had never studied the final moments of life and had never seen it discussed in a book. I was sure that the process of death was fully described in medical textbooks, but he said it wasn't. I went to two major medical school libraries where, with the help of the reference librarians, I conducted a computer search of thousands of books. The topics included internal medicine, primary care, gerontology, intensive care, and hospice care, but none of them described the process of death. We found a few books whose titles suggested that they examined the physical aspects of death, but they were written in the sixteenth or seventeenth centuries. Even the nursing textbooks contained little information on death. This surprised me, for I had thought that nurses would see a fair amount of death and would have to be formally prepared. It appears, however, that death has not been written about at length. When it has been discussed, it is as a footnote to the failure of a body system or organ. There are countless books on the psychological aspects of death, but the physical aspects are apparently overlooked. Those who do know the events of death most likely learned of them by watching a loved one die.

This chapter looks at the physical process of death. I don't talk about the internal, biochemical events. Instead, I describe some of the things that you will see, hear, feel, and smell as someone dies. This information may make you uncomfortable, and you certainly don't have to read it. Skip ahead to the next chapter if you prefer not to know.

THE MYTH OF DEATH

Few people have a peaceful death or die in their sleep, perhaps just enough to keep the myth alive. The reality of death is harsher. Many dying people appear to be struggling toward the end, as if the body and the soul that have been intertwined for so many years do not want to let go of each other. It is often terribly painful for us to watch this struggle. Yet, the moment the struggle has ended, most people in the room will feel as if the body and soul have now gone their individual ways and are at peace.

Dying is like shutting down a large factory filled with engines and assembly lines and giant boilers. Everything does not suddenly go quiet when the "off" switch is pushed. Instead, the machinery creaks and moans as it slows to a halt. Unless suddenly felled by an accident, a heart attack, or other sudden trauma, most of our bodies are like those factories, creaking and moaning as they shut down. It can be difficult to remember that the winding-down process is natural. We do not go gently into death, to paraphrase Dylan Thomas's words. No matter how prepared we think we are for death, we do not let go of life easily. We "rage, rage," in Thomas's words, "against the dying of the light."

Death is as primitive as birth. Often loud and messy, it is always deeply authentic. We can find peace and dignity in this authenticity.

THE PEACE OF DEATH

The struggle that appears to engulf the dying is often referred to as the "agonal" phase of death, for many people appear to be in agony at the end. Yet many researchers believe that at the end of life the body releases endorphins, special hormones that block pain and give one a sense of tranquillity and joy. When told that they appeared to be in great pain, many people who have had near-death experiences have said that they actually had been at peace.

I was once told about astronauts who took part in tests to determine how many gravity forces, called "Gs," the body can withstand. At a certain point in these physically punishing tests, the astronauts passed out. This is as close to a death experience as we can simulate. When questioned about how they felt, the astronauts said that despite looking as if they were in agony and despite undergoing a terrible physical trauma, they were actually euphoric.

This is a difficult phenomenon to prove, yet many trauma workers report that it appears to be true. I was driving to work early one rainy morning before sunrise. Few cars were on the road. For no apparent reason, the station wagon in front of me lost control and drove head-on into a large tree. I quickly rushed to the car in the darkness and pulled open the door to expose one of the most horrific sights I have ever seen. There was a woman in her late twenties, covered with blood, her body so mangled that I couldn't tell the color of her skin. I looked down and saw something coming out of the dashboard. It appeared to be stabbing her in her right hip. Then I realized that her femur, the upper bone of the leg, had been ripped from her body and was jammed into the dashboard. Her breathing was severely labored. After what seemed to be an eternity, but was probably only a second or two, I realized that I would not be able to remove her from the car, and that she was going to die. A shout from the house across the street told me that someone had called 911. All I could do was to be with her until help arrived.

During the time I sat with her, I thought about how young she was and how severely her body had been damaged. I saw toys and a baby seat in the backseat, and realized that this young mother was not going to see her baby grow up. She seemed to be aware of what was happening. She was losing everything, yet she had a serene look on her face, she did not rage; she followed death peacefully into the night.

Although any certainty regarding death is elusive, I believe that we die in peace. The separation of body and soul looks painful to us, the survivors, but I believe it is not so difficult for the one who is passing. Like the factory machinery slowing to a stop, the body moans and creaks, but internally it is at peace.

WHY WE DIE

Old age, terminal diseases, and life-ending traumas eventually become roads taking us to predictable endpoints. Organs and body systems become like dominoes falling upon one another. The order of failure depends on the underlying disease or trauma, as well as on the person's general health, previous ailments, medical care, and other factors. We approach the final stage of the journey as the circulatory system fails, the brain can no longer coordinate life-support systems, one or more organs give up the struggle, the body tissues are no longer receiving enough oxygen, or entire body systems are destroyed.

No matter where the disease, trauma, or deterioration begins in the body, no matter which part of the body suffers first or most, death does not occur until the heart fails to beat and one is no longer breathing. Death is usually defined as an irreversible cessation of brain, respiratory system, and circulatory system function. But some of the states that occur in this definition of death happen in situations that do not lead to death. For example, doctors can use electrical paddles to "shock" stalled hearts into beating on their own again. The respiratory failure that occurs with drowning may be temporary and reversible with CPR. The circulatory system can fail, for example, if you suffer massive trauma and extensive blood loss. However, the problem can be reversed with blood transfusions and other measures. And while the brain can survive only a few minutes without oxygen, prompt restoration of the oxygen will prevent permanent damage. For death to occur, the failure of the brain, respiratory, and circulatory systems must be *irreversible*.

WHEN WE DIE

Friends and family often spend days with loved ones whose conditions are deteriorating. Many have other obligations like working and taking care of children, but they still want desperately to be present when death is near. While there is no guaranteed way to know when death is close, or to predict the moment of death, there are several common signs of approaching death.

Kathy, a woman in her late thirties, had the misfortune of contracting AIDS. Previously a governmental relations specialist, she became an AIDS activist, fighting for the rights of the afflicted, lobbying to have more money spent on AIDS research and treatment. People marveled at her energy, but they were even more impressed by her unfailing sense of humor. She was the life of every party, with a unique, ironic way of looking at life.

Her family and friends, myself included, gathered at her bedside. We knew that death was near but did not know if the final moment would come in the next minutes, hours, or days. Kathy was expected to die during the weekend, but Monday morning we were still at her bedside. Most of us had to go to work or take care of our families, so we left, gathering again at lunchtime. Kathy's condition was unchanged.

We ordered a pizza, Kathy's favorite food, and sat at her bedside, talking to her, holding her hands, comforting her and each other. All of a sudden Kathy took a turn for the worse. Her breathing became deep and difficult, more pronounced and labored than it had previously been, letting us know that death was arriving. At the exact moment death took Kathy, the pizza arrived. Shocked, we stood silently for many moments. Finally someone opened the door, paid for the pizza, and sent the stunned delivery person on his way. There was nothing left to do but eat the pizza in her honor, celebrating Kathy's characteristic sense of timing.

WHAT HAPPENS AS WE DIE

These are the common signs of impending death. This is not meant to be a textbook discussion, simply an explanation of what to expect. Not all of these events will occur in every death, and there is no set order of events. Even though a body may be ravaged by disease, there is still an innate force of life that pushes the body to continue, almost as if it doesn't realize that its time has come. That's why it is often not as easy to die as you might expect. Many times, I've been surprised at how hard it is for a body to die.

SLEEPING

Sleeping usually increases in the days and hours preceding death; it's almost as if the body is withdrawing from life. There may be no single cause for the tremendous increase in sleeping, other than the fact that many body systems have shut down or slipped into low gear. One widespread but unproved theory states that one sleeps so much because the body is conserving energy, shunting what energy it has left only to the most vital organs.

As death approaches, this increase in sleeping can build to a comalike state of unresponsiveness—the person cannot be awakened. If this is a significant change, it is a good idea to mention it to the physician. But the increased sleeping is usually just nature taking its course, and all we can do is make the dying person as comfortable as possible.

EATING

Food and beverage intake generally decrease in the final stage of life. We're tempted to force food on the dying, thinking that everything would be all right if we could just get them to eat something. We're also afraid that they will die of starvation or thirst. But the inability or refusal to eat and drink is only a symptom of the larger problem, the one that will take them away from us.

Never give food or drink to a sleeping or unconscious person—you might accidentally cause her to choke. If her lips are dry or she is awake and thirsty but cannot tolerate fluids, you can wet her lips with ice or lemon glycerin swabs, which are available at drugstores or from the nurses' station.

INCONTINENCE

There may be loss of bladder and bowel control. This may make the dying physically uncomfortable as well as frightened and embarrassed. We can place absorbent pads under them for comfort and cleanliness. We can lovingly reassure them and protect their privacy as much as possible. The doctor may have ordered a catheter, if incontinence of urine has been an ongoing problem. Toward the end of life, less food and water in the body will result in fewer bowel movements and less urination. Urine output will drop further as the kidneys shut down.

BREATHING

Among the most noticeable and disturbing changes associated with the approach of death are the changes in breathing. Breathing is a subtle noise, one we're accustomed to hearing in the background if at all. When it is pronounced, strained, or uneven, it can be frightening to the observer.

Some may continue breathing fairly normally until almost the end, while others may struggle for each breath for hours or days. If a person has lung cancer or another respiratory disease, the distress may continue for weeks or months. I have been in many homes and hospital rooms that were dominated by loud, rasping breathing that almost seemed to suck the walls in closer with each inhalation and force them back with every exhalation. In other situations, it's the sudden lack of breathing that scares us.

There are many breathing patterns associated with imminent demise, including dyspnea, apnea, and Cheyne-Stokes.

Dyspnea is a complaint defined as labored breathing and short breaths. Simply taking a breath seems to be a great effort. With each inhalation, the skin on the side of the belly, just below the lungs, seems to get sucked up behind the bottom rib.

If our loved ones are still awake and alert at this point, dyspnea can greatly frighten them. They feel as if they can't get enough air, which is one of the most frightening experiences we can face. I remember sitting in a children's hospital one night, watching sixteen-year-old Jeremy struggle to breathe during his final hours of life. The handsome youngster, who had fought so valiantly against cystic fibrosis, was now close to death and still alert. He was terrified, and there was nothing his family and I could do but hold his hands, make sure he was getting enough pain medication, and tell him that he was loved and safe. As we sat with him through the night, we talked about what Marianne Williamson wrote in her book *Illuminata:* "I used to think that the Angel of Death would be a terrible thing. I realize now that the Angel of Death would have to be God's most tender and understanding Angel, to be sent to us at such a significant, frightening juncture."

If your loved one appears to be in pain, ask the doctor for medication. If he is anxious, the doctor may prescribe additional medicine; perhaps morphine, which helps with both the pain and the anxiety. But sometimes the best medicine is to let the patient know that he is loved and not alone.

Apnea is a period of no breathing that lasts for between one and sixty seconds. Caused by a decrease in circulation and a buildup of the body's waste products, apnea strikes for brief periods at first. Then the episodes of nonbreathing get longer as the body winds down. It may start days or only minutes before death. Apnea can be very startling. We may think our loved one has passed, only to jump as breathing restarts with a loud, gasping breath. The onset of apnea is often a clue that the end is near. There's nothing we can do to make our loved ones more comfortable when apnea strikes. Indeed, it's often more uncomfortable for us to watch than it is for them to experience, for they are unconscious. The best thing we can do at this time is to stay near our loved one and comfort one another.

Cheyne-Stokes breathing is a rhythmic waxing and waning of the breathing which may alternate with periods of apnea. This irregular pattern of breathing begins with slow, shallow breaths. Breathing becomes faster and deeper, building in intensity until the breathing is perhaps as hard and fast as someone engaged in strenuous activity. Then there is a period of no breathing (apnea) for one to sixty seconds, and the cycle repeats itself. You'll hear the breathing building, becoming loud and gaspy, then all will be quiet. This may be an indication that death is near. As is the case with all these breathing changes, the best thing to do is to make sure the doctor has been notified and your loved one is comfortable.

CYANOSIS

A lack of oxygen in the blood, coupled with an increase in carbon dioxide, can result in a bluish discoloration of the skin and mucous membranes (such as the lips) called cyanosis. The skin and mucous membranes don't actually turn blue. Rather, there is a hint of blue or blue-gray. Cyanosis may appear before death as the circulatory system is impaired. But since our loved ones are usually close to death at this point and are unaware of the cyanosis, it is typically only the care-givers who notice the change. Remember that this is a normal part of the dying process.

HYPOXIA

As the ability to take in oxygen and circulate it through-out the body decreases, many parts of the body may suffer oxygen deficiency. There may be behavioral changes, poor judgment, decreased alertness, headaches, increased drowsiness, and other symptoms. Hypoxia can also lead to convulsions, unresponsiveness, and, in advanced stages, to cyanosis. It is important to make sure that the dying person is safe and is receiving medications that may help to relieve headaches or other symptoms. Remember that their judgment may be impaired in case any decisions need to be made.

CONVULSIONS

Body cells communicate by passing electrical impulses to each other. This communication falters as we near death. Blood pressure falls, causing the oxygen supply to the brain to drop and brain cells to malfunction. The cells spontaneously fire off electrical discharges, causing an electrical storm in the brain, shooting out random and purposeless commands to various parts of the body. This is a convulsion.

Many lives end in a sudden convulsion—the arms and legs shake, the jaw tightens, and the person may seem to be undergoing an epileptic seizure. The shaking sometimes seems to move from the stomach to the top of the body. All we can do is make sure that our loved ones are safe, and will not hurt themselves. Since this often happens just before death, it is a good time to gently caress our loved ones, reassuring them that they are safe and loved, whether they can hear us or not.

ODOR

The decay of flesh that may occur if the body can no longer nourish its tissue or keep it healthy produces a characteristic foul odor. The smell is of necrotic tissue, which means tissue that is dying. With cancer, flesh dies because cancer cells are poorly organized and not properly vascularized—meaning they do not receive an adequate blood supply.

Those with diabetes or other conditions in which parts of the body do not receive adequate blood flow may find the tissue in those parts of the body slowly dying, producing an odor. It is hard to describe or compare this odor to other smells. The odor is more common in those with cancer, especially of the lung, mouth, or esophagus. Unfortunately, there's no easy remedy. Most people acclimate to the smell within a few minutes. Others have found that air fresheners or opening a window, if possible, may help.

FEVER AND SWEATING

Fever is very common toward the end, as the body attempts to fight off massive infections. Our loved ones will sometimes sweat profusely, as if they are engaging in a major struggle. Like many other things that happen at this stage, medical treatment will not help. The best thing we can do is lovingly wipe their brows.

RESTLESSNESS

I recently spent time with an elderly man named Louis, who was struggling with terminal colon cancer that had spread throughout his abdomen. In the later stages of dying, Louis had great difficulty breathing and was in pain. Both he and his family were tremendously frustrated by his inability to find a comfortable position in which to sit or lie. His abdomen felt better when he lay down, but then he had difficulty breathing. Sitting up made breathing easier, but increased the abdominal pain.

Restlessness is often a part of the transition. People will tug on their sheets, constantly turn over in bed, stand up and sit down, ask you to raise or lower the heads of their beds, and so on. The difficulty in finding a comfortable position may be caused by respiratory distress, by pain, by anxiety, or any number of other factors. And it may not be that they simply haven't found the "right" position yet—sometimes there is no right position.

We can help by adjusting our loved one's positions as frequently as necessary. If this condition continues for a long period of time, the doctor may prescribe a sedative to calm our loved one. It is important to make sure that the restlessness is not caused by an underlying pain. This is a good time to do a pain reassessment.

THE HEART

Unless one has had a heart attack or the heart is otherwise the primary focus of the disease, the heart often works harder toward the end, trying to compensate for the failure of other organs and systems. If, for example, there isn't enough oxygen in the blood, the heart pumps harder and faster.

The heart's attempt is valiant, but the increased heart rate (called tachycardia) can't make up for the lack of oxygen in the blood. When the exhausted heart can no longer continue it may slow down, continuing to slow until it beats no more. Because of the determined heart, many AIDS patients continue to hang on to life despite the complete devastation of their bodies. People with AIDS are typically young and their still-strong hearts are unaffected by the HIV virus. It seems very cruel for the virus to prolong the final phase of life by ignoring the heart, which beats on bravely.

CIRCULATION

Blood circulation slows as the body begins to fade. You can see the results of slow circulation by touching your loved one's hands and feet. You'll notice that they're colder than usual.

When circulation has been severely compromised and the heart can no longer pump blood throughout the body, you can see a dark, maroon-colored discoloration on the underside of the patient's body. The blood, which is no longer pumped vigorously through the arteries and veins, is pulled to the lowest part of the body by gravity, where it pools.

In many cases the blood-clotting mechanism will fail, leading to spontaneous bleeding in different parts of the body. You'll notice unexplained bruises at various points in the body. What the person is doing may have no effect on the bruises. She may be lying quietly on her back, yet suddenly develop a bruise on her chest. People have asked about special, soft mattresses, which in other circumstances may prevent bedsores or skin discomfort. However, they will probably make no difference during the dying process, and trying to change our loved one's mattress at this time will most likely bring the individual more discomfort than comfort. This is also a good time for a pain reassessment.

THE EYES

The brain has higher and lower centers of functioning. The higher centers control speaking, thinking, and other cognitive processes. Lower centers automatically regulate our breathing, heartbeat, senses, and other functions without our having to think about them. One of these lower functions is the pupillary reflex or light reflex, the eye's reaction to light. Light entering the eyes is projected onto the retina, and a signal is sent to the brain via the optical nerve. The brain responds by commanding the muscles of the eye to react to the light by expanding or constricting. This is called the light reflex. If the part of the brain which controls the light reflex has ceased to function, the eyes may become dilated. For the same reason, the eyes may also become fixed (no longer moving). The eyes will no longer follow if the head is turned. This is sometimes referred to as "doll's eyes," giving the face a lifeless appearance.

Once the eyes, the windows to the soul, have become lifeless, it seems as if our loved one has departed.

VISION AND HEARING

Along with the other senses, hearing and vision decrease. As vision fades, people will remark that things seem blurry or dim. Yet, as they see less of this world, some people appear to begin looking into the world to come. It's not unusual for the dying to have visions, often of someone who has already passed on. Your father may tell you that Aunt Betty visited him last night, or he might speak to Betty as if she were there in the room, at that moment.

There's really no point in telling your father that he is hallucinating, that Betty's dead and can't possibly be there. For all we know, the veil that separates life and death may lift in the last moments of life, and your father may be more in touch with that world than with ours. And if Aunt Betty is not there, well, does it matter?

Instead of arguing ask him, "What is Betty saying? Tell me more about your vision." Perhaps Betty is telling your father that it's okay to die, or maybe they're laughing about the time they went to the circus.

I've heard people say to their loved ones: "It's great that Betty is here with you," or "I knew that Mother would come to meet you," or "I'm so glad Jeff will be with you during the trip."

One woman, Dorothy, had unfinished business with her

husband, Ralph. As Ralph lay at death's door, unresponsive, Dorothy shook him and shouted in his ear: "I love you! Do you love me?" When he did not answer, she shook him harder and shouted louder until she realized that he could no longer communicate with her.

We have no way of actually testing one's hearing at this stage, although we do have anecdotal information from people who have been in comas or had near-death experiences. Many of them report being able to hear during these times. It is widely believed that hearing is one of the last senses to go, which is why medical professionals are taught to behave as if patients can hear right up to the end.

When people ask me if their loved ones can still hear them, I tell them "Yes. If not physically, then they can hear you spiritually. They may not be alert, but I believe that if you have something to truly say from your heart, they can truly hear from theirs."

SHOUTING

It is not unusual for a dying person to let out a loud yell that seems to come from deep within at the moment of death. It's not so much a word as it is a sound. This is more of a reflex than an attempt to communicate. I don't believe that they are in pain as much as undergoing a physical spasm involving the voice box and lungs in their final protest against the separation of body and soul. There is nothing to do except be with our loved one at this time.

DEATH RATTLE

Loved ones gathered by the bed are always deeply disturbed to hear what is commonly known as the "death rattle." The sound usually results from the body's inability to clear or cough up saliva or other secretions which may collect in the back of the throat, lungs or upper airways. Our instinct is to do something, for we fear our loved one is drowning in his own secretions. I often tell people that it sounds worse than it actually is. It is helpful to realize that this is the sound of air passing through water, much like the sound you hear when you are finishing up a can of soda with a straw. Air still gets through to the lungs. Knowing that this is simply part of the body's process of shutting down helps to relieve our anxiety. It may also be an indication that death is near.

FOAM AT THE MOUTH

It is common for a little bit of foaming at the mouth to occur at the time of death. This is a natural occurrence.

I worked with a loving woman who was very protective of her husband. She had spent her entire adult life trying to give him a nice home and family, always presenting herself at her best. Even dying and in pain, she was more concerned about how her death would affect her husband than she was about herself. In fact, she had asked me to "shoo him out of the room if any embarrassing or undignified thing happened. I don't want the last image he has of me to be my diaper being changed."

Her husband was sleeping in a chair by her bed when she died. As people often do, she foamed at the mouth in those last moments. I felt that this woman who was so concerned about her husband's well-being would not want him to see her like this, so I wiped the foam away, preserving her dignity in death, and then woke him.

WHEN DEATH HAS OCCURRED

When life has passed out of your loved one's body, there will be no breathing and no heartbeat. She won't respond when you speak to her or touch her. Her eyelids will be slightly open and her eyes fixed, as if staring straight ahead. Her jaw will be relaxed and slightly open. Her skin will have lost its glow, its color and tenacity; that intangible force that once inflated it will be gone. Whenever I have seen someone who has just passed away, it seems to me as if their body has been turned off. The intangible current of life is most obvious when it is no longer present.

Even though watching someone physically die is an emotionally painful experience, most people feel as if they have shared a precious and profound moment with their loved one.

Take your time. Many people believe that the spirit is still close to the body immediately after death. Talk to her. Hold her hands. Caress her. Pray for her. Wish her well on her journey. Do what feels right for you. Even though the physical connection has just ended, the emotional connection continues.

9

DYING IN THE
EYE OF THE STORM

The right to die in peace and dignity.
The right to die.
The right to participate in all decisions concerning one's
  care.
The right to be treated as a living human being.

When I was nine years old, my family was living down South where hurricanes are a summer event. Every year there are new storms with new names but the same preparations and fears. In 1969, Hurricane Camille changed my world forever. We spent the night under the steel porch of the elementary school gym. It was the loudest night of my life. I mostly remember the noise, the crashing sounds, the howling winds. I knew that there was death and destruction in that noise, and that somewhere out there cries for help were going unheeded. Then, suddenly, there was nothing. No wind, no rain, no sound. Complete peace and silence. We were in the eye of the storm. As the storm moved past us the winds started up again, this time from the opposite direction. As the howling and crashing sounds returned, we wondered how we could possibly survive the night.

This is our challenge: To find peace and dignity in death and dying. To cope with situations that make us feel as if we're being pounded from all angles, and with problems that subtly diminish us as well. Our peace and dignity are not suddenly taken away at once. The process begins in small ways.

Mrs. Hanson is a friendly, intelligent woman in her mid-sixties with a high-grade brain tumor. She was spending her last days in the hospice unit of a hospital near her home. While we were visiting her one day, a nurse came into the room to change her IV bag.

"How are you today, sweet cakes?" the nurse asked brightly.

"Please call me 'whole wheat,'" Mrs. Hanson replied sweetly.

That puzzled the nurse. "Why 'whole wheat'?" she asked.

"Why 'sweet cakes'?" shot back Mrs. Hanson.

Mrs. Hanson used humor to let the nurse know by not using her name she was taking away her dignity. We spend our entire lives searching for our dignity, trying to discover who we are and how we want to live. We find our dignity and simultaneously show it to all in the way we live our lives. Living with dignity is living life in a way that matters, seeing ourselves as being worthy, and bringing that great sense of self-worth to everything we do. Ultimately, it has nothing to do with how we earn our living or where we live.

Just as we have the right to live with dignity, we have the right to die with dignity. Dying with dignity means knowing that your death will be just as meaningful and purposeful as your life has been. It means dying the way *you* want to die, not the way others have deemed proper or worthy for you. Dying with dignity means being you, just as you have always been, right up to the end.

LOSS OF DIGNITY

Far too many of us are forced to struggle to maintain our dignity as our lives close. The greatest thief of dignity is the medical system, which strips away dignity by depersonalizing us and turning us from people with lives, histories, and families into room numbers and beds with conditions. To some doctors and nurses you're not Mrs. Hanson, the woman who lost her husband in a car accident, then went to college at night and opened her own business, all while raising three children. Instead, you're "the brain tumor in 644" or "the heart failure in Room 302." It's hard to maintain your dignity when you're defined and described as a disease and a room number.

The system robs us of dignity by treating disease and death as the enemy, insisting that they be stamped out at all costs! Our bodies become battlefields where doctors fight to "fix us." We don't like to acknowledge that life is sometimes uncomfortable, or even downright unpleasant. And when we're broken, we want them to fix us. We want to believe that we can fix everything. But we can't fix the dying because they're not broken. Dying is not failing; it's a normal part of life.

Even when trying to help maintain dignity, the medical system can take it away. When I talk to medical and nursing students about death, I often ask them to write down how they would like to die—where they want to be, who should be there, whether or not they will request heroic measures, what they will be wearing, even what music might be playing. Then I tell them: "Look at what you've written. These death scenes you've planned for yourselves are what you will soon be projecting on your patients. If you want to die with soft music playing and incense in the air, that's your right. But don't insist that your patients do the same. If they want to die in peace or in chaos, with rock music or soft music, that's their right. To force your beliefs on them is to rob them of their right to choose, and ultimately, their dignity."

The medical system is not the only thing that robs the dying of their dignity. Caring loved ones who try to get them to do the "right thing" are also unknowingly at fault. The "right thing" may be moving back home when they'd rather stay in their own apartments. It may be for them to rest all day when they'd really rather spend their remaining time with friends. It may be to watch the news and keep up with current events when they no longer care what's happening in the world. It may be for them to fight the disease when they have decided to pass on in peace. It doesn't matter what the "right thing" is. If they're forced to accept it, their dignity has been assaulted.

Finally, the dying unwittingly rob themselves of dignity when they forget what really matters. The process of death is by nature one of loss. They lose, among other things, the "outer layers" accumulated during life. They are no longer the chairman of the board or the friendly neighbor or the baseball buddy or the great Cajun cook. They let go of the roles of leader, teacher, worker, friend, athlete, mother, father, son, daughter, brother, and sister. The roles in which they took such pride during their lifetimes slip away as they're thrust into the role of the patient. What are they left with? The way they see themselves. If they see themselves as being special and unique, above and apart from those worldly roles, then they retain their dignity. This is easy for some people to do, for their dignity is defined solely from within. Others need reinforcement from their loved ones and the medical system. That's why it is so important for those close to the dying to treat them with dignity.

Honesty, Respect, Compassion

I remember meeting a young man in his late thirties suffering from Lou Gehrig's disease (amyotrophic lateral sclerosis). He was awaiting death in the hospital, and no one knew how many days or weeks he had remaining. As we spoke late one evening, after his wife and children had left, I asked him, "What's the toughest part of this experience?"

"Most people would think it's the physical decline," he answered immediately. "But it's not. And it's not being in the hospital—this place is fine. The nurses are very kind and attentive, the doctor is great about explaining the disease and what lies ahead for me. My family visits all the time, the food is fine, I have cable TV. *But the hardest part for me is I feel like I'm being seen in the past tense.* Something that *once was* complete and important. And I *used* to be the energetic father, the loving husband, the best photographer in town. No one could capture a moment on film like I could. I can't do all that anymore but I'm still me. I am still complete. Even if the day comes that I can't feed myself anymore, I want to be treated as a whole person. I don't want anyone to look down on me, to treat me like a baby or half a person."

Whether we're loved ones, friends, or health care workers, we owe the dying exactly what we owe the living, for they are fully alive and living right up until the end: honesty, respect, and compassion. We owe them the opportunity to be true to themselves, to discover death in their own ways, and to die in their own ways. We owe the dying our love and our respect. We have an obligation to help them live and die with dignity, with their heads held high right up to the end.

In some cases we don't have to do anything to help them maintain their dignity, for it is defined from within. Other people, however, draw at least part of their dignity from they way they are seen and treated by others. Protecting their dignity may mean addressing them by their proper names, until given permission to use a first name or nickname. It may mean knocking before entering their room. It may mean asking them what they want to happen and listening carefully to the answers. It may not be *what* you do so much as *how* you do it and how you think of them, for what you think is always reflected in the tone of your voice and in your actions.

Believing that the dying are fully alive and deserving of respect is in itself treating them with dignity. They *are* fully alive and deserving of our respect. The only difference is that now they need our help. We have an opportunity to provide that help, not as an obligation, but as a privilege.

THE RIGHT TO DIE WITH DIGNITY

Society's concept of the right to die is controversial and evolving. When the right to die was mentioned a few years ago, most people immediately thought of the Karen Anne Quinlan story. To many people at that time, the right to die meant not being kept alive by artificial means such as feeding tubes and respirators. But when we mention the right to die today, assisted suicide springs to most minds. A discussion of both of these aspects of the right to die is warranted.

Rightly or wrongly, Dr. Jack Kevorkian has forced the issue of assisted death to the forefront: whether or not physicians should be allowed to assist in the deaths of terminally ill patients. The real question is not *should* health care workers assist in death; it is whether we come to grips with what has been going on since the beginning of medicine.

Most physicians over the age of thirty have participated in some nonverbal way in hastening a patient's death, as an act of compassion and a way to end suffering. Every health care worker has heard the stories passed around at the hospitals. I remember hearing one about a woman with multiple myeloma back in the 1950s. She was so riddled with the cancer that her bones cracked when she was moved, her ribs broke when she was turned over. She spent most of her time in a drug-induced haze, moaning loudly. One day the young doctor who cared for her at the county hospital found her in a deep, apparently peaceful sleep, which was very unusual. When he questioned the senior doctors, they told him to be quiet and to let well enough alone. The young doctor later learned that the woman had finally been given the "little extra medicine" she had been pleading for, as "an act of mercy."

Doctors have found other ways of assisting death. In the early 1960s, before the advent of intensive care and coronary care units, if a patient was in distress he was immediately given intravenous fluids to push up his blood pressure. Then the doctors would evaluate the situation and decide how to proceed. But sometimes the doctor made a little hand signal to the nurse. It was an unspoken but clear message: Turn off the IV. There was also the "Code Blue" approach. Doctors ran to the patient's room when a "Code Blue" was broadcast over the hospital's public address system. The patient's family was quickly ushered out of the room as the doctors began to work on saving the patient's life. But sometimes the physicians did a "slow code," standing around waiting for the patient to die, rather than needlessly prolonging a life that would only continue in an irreversibly vegetative or intractably painful state. This can't be done today, for there are too many people present at codes, with one person assigned to document everything said and done. Still, there are other ways in which doctors can, and undoubtedly do, assist a patient in dying. They can simply stop asking certain questions or not order certain tests. In other words, they can subtly ease back on the patient's care, allowing nature to take its course.

Assisted death and assisted suicide have been going on all along. But why should these decisions be left in the hands of doctors, operating surreptitiously, often not really knowing their patients' wishes? We should be able to make that decision by ourselves, perhaps in consultation with our loved ones and to have our loved ones present at our final moments. The battle over the issue of whether one has the right to terminate one's own life or to be assisted in doing so by a physician or loved one is being waged in our courts. In 1996, for the first time in history, a federal appeals court ruled that a mentally competent, terminally ill adult has a constitutional right to hasten his own death. In the ruling, Judge Stephen Reinhardt of Los Angeles noted that "a competent, terminally ill adult having lived nearly the full measure of his life, has a strong liberty interest in choosing a dignified and humane death rather than being reduced at the end of his existence to a childlike state of helplessness, diapered, sedated, incompetent." In his provocative ruling, the judge went on to say, "The decision how and when to die is one of the most intimate and personal choices a person may make in a lifetime, a choice central to personal dignity and autonomy."

The law says that we can't have any help doing so, we can't have someone stand by to hold our hands or assist us in ending our own life. Simply being present is legally dangerous for loved ones and doctors, so most stay away.

How many people commit suicide in solitude rather than

risk having their loved ones prosecuted if they ask for help? How many simply want someone to hold their hand as they pass on? The true numbers are unknown, but we do know of individual cases. Some of these cases were recently reported in a *Los Angeles Times* article. Elvin and his wife, Sara, had been married for forty-nine years. During the last eleven years, Sara suffered from a heart condition that became so painful she could barely speak. Her doctors could offer no hope, no way out of the pain, so Sara decided to end her life. "On the day of her decision," Elvin said, "I was with her up to the point of placing the bag over her head and she said, 'Elvin, you must go to the office because you cannot be implicated in this.' She had to die alone. I was denied my right to be with her when she died. This is not right . . . a person has the right to control the conditions of their death as much as they have the right to control the conditions of their living."

Many husbands, wives, companions, children, and siblings have ignored the law, and found themselves on trial for doing so. When fifty-four-year-old James Northcutt, a renowned interior designer, decided to end his battle with AIDS, he asked his doctor for help in dying. The doctor refused. So James, practically blind from complications of AIDS, suffering from painful neuropathy, diarrhea, nausea, fever, and many other problems, down to only 110 pounds, checked himself out of the hospital and went home to die. On December 4, 1995, he took over 100 pills, then went down to the garage. There, he ran a hose from the exhaust pipe of his BMW back into the car itself. He was intent on dying. After a tearful good-bye, his partner, Keith Green, watched him enter the running car. Upon leaving, Keith noticed that the tape holding up the pipe was slipping, so he pushed it back down with his hand. He reluctantly left his companion of eight years to die alone.

Keith got in his car and drove off. He was supposed to stay away but couldn't. After just a few minutes he returned home, called the authorities, then sat in the car amid all the smoke. Jim was most likely dead by the time his life-partner returned, but Keith sat with him, holding his hand. "I just wanted to hold his hand," Keith says, "I just didn't want him to be alone."

For Keith, helping James die and holding his hand as he did so, was an act of love. For the authorities, it was an act of murder. Despite the fact that James had left eight notarized suicide notes and other documents threatening to sue anyone who resuscitated him, the authorities arrested Keith Green for murder. As a result of the charges, Keith was not allowed to go to his companion's funeral or to return to the home they had shared for many years. During the legal battle, the district attorneys offered to drop the charges against Keith if he volunteered for 300 hours in an AIDS hospice, an ironic offer for someone accused of murder and assisted suicide. Keith refused, preferring to stand up for the right to help a loved one suffering from disease and pain to die with dignity. The case was resolved when charges were dropped six months later, after the coroner ruled that James had been killed by the pills, not the exhaust fumes.

Is there a midpoint between forcing our loved ones to place a bag over their heads, dying all alone on the one hand, and charging someone with murder if they push the tape down on the other? While there is no answer to this serious societal dilemma, it is important to point out that this is not a new concept. As a society, we have decided it is humane to put pets to sleep rather than see them suffer from an incurable disease. No one insists that there is any value in a pet's continued suffering. Now we must decide about one another: Is there a point at which we can agree? As individuals we must look within ourselves, our families, and to our religious leaders, and as a society we must instruct our legislatures and courts to find and agree upon that midpoint. For many, there is no midpoint.

The other aspect of the right to die, the right not to be kept alive by artificial means, brings up one of our greatest terrors: being trapped. A century ago, the fear of being buried alive was widespread. More than a few people were declared dead before their time, giving rise to the terrible fear that one would wake from a deep coma to find oneself lying in a dark closed box, breathing fleeting air, listening to the sounds of dirt being thrown on top of the box from above. Pipes were sometimes run from the coffin up to the open air when one was buried so that if the "deceased" was still alive, he could get air and scream for help. An alarm system was also used. If someone woke up inside a coffin they could pull on a string which would ring a bell perched above their grave.

When technology improved we could tell exactly when life ended: If there was no heartbeat, there was no life. But technology leapt further ahead, and we can now keep people "alive" with machines that take over for organs that no longer function. So today we do not fear being buried too soon; we fear being kept alive too long.

Death was more humane in the past. In most cases people simply lay down and eventually "melted into the bed." It became more complex as technology progressed but left doctors room to make hard decisions. Was it fair for physicians to make those decisions without consulting the patients or their families? Today, doctors have much less leeway. They go to the other extreme, keeping people alive at any cost. Many, in fact, insist on "going by the book" in every instance, and by the most conservative book imaginable, lest they be sued or lose their licenses. We are forced to face the difficult questions.

Harold's mother suffered a major stroke that left her partially paralyzed, unable to speak or eat. She had said she did not want to be kept alive with a feeding tube, but her family reluctantly agreed to one after her hospital threatened legal action. Harold described what happened to his mother: "Over the next two months, Mom removed the feeding tube about a dozen times. It was reinserted each time, a very unpleasant procedure which required a physician and X ray. To prevent further removal of the tube, her unparalyzed left hand was tied to the bedrail. However . . . she was able to move herself slowly so she could reach the tube with her tethered left hand and remove it, which she did repeatedly. In February, at her doctor's suggestion, a 'jejunal' feeding tube was surgically put into her stomach through her abdomen. Mom mercifully passed away in early March after having been, in effect, tortured to death while being treated contrary to her expressly stated wishes."

Is there a midpoint between forcing people to accept painful care they wish to avoid and letting them die from lack of care? We want people to die naturally, but is it natural to be kept "alive" in a coma on a respirator, receiving predigested amino acids through a nasal tube into the stomach? Something has gone wrong with the medical community when it refers to withdrawing artificial technological support, feeding tubes, and respirators as "killing" our loved ones.

In many cases technology does nothing more than

increase the length and depth of suffering at the end of life. If lengthening life were the only goal, then staying "alive" forever on a respirator would be a wonderful thing. But if quality of life is considered at all, there may be a time to say no. We must find ways to decrease the suffering brought about by technology. We must learn to make the distinction between ending suffering and ending life. Not to intervene in cases where the battle has already been lost is not cruel; it is humane.

The right to die is vital: Forcing you to stay alive beyond your days robs you of your dignity.

DIGNIFIED DYING

Late one afternoon an orderly entered the room of Mrs. Hanson, who didn't want to be called "sweet cakes," to find the summer sun beating on the window. He said, "Let's close these curtains, I know you don't want this afternoon sun." She called the orderly to her bedside and said: "This is my death. You die your way, I'll die mine." She was honest and authentic up to the end, and she was dignified.

Emergency room physician Mark Katz has a compassionate approach to preserving dignity: "I remember the first cardiac arrest I saw, when I was an intern, being very haphazard, with everyone flailing around. Today, I try to keep the energy of a cardiac code soft yet thorough. Once the patient is intubated and has an IV line, once you're giving medications, doing CPR and occasionally defibrillating, the whole thing can become very peaceful. I try to talk calmly yet firmly so things do not get crazy when we have a cardiac arrest here. If we have done everything possible without any success, a person should pass out of life with as much dignity as possible.

And we can give them that dignity by having a dignified response to their cardiac arrest."

For Aileen Getty, dying with dignity means something special: "Those people around me accepting my dying and honoring it. No longer honoring the past and talking about the past, but honoring my future. That would enhance my dying."

Lawrence described what he considered to be a dignified death. In his mid- to late thirties, Lawrence has Hodgkin's disease. One afternoon, over coffee, I asked him if he had thought about his own death and dignity. He replied: "I've thought a lot about how I want to die. I want to be involved in my death, I want to have control over it. I want to be surrounded by people I know and love. I want to die somewhere nice, at home or a friend's house, with the wind blowing and the sun shining. I wouldn't be afraid of ending it sooner, instead of lingering in pain. There's no dignity in letting disease show you its worst face. Why not say some nice 'good-byes' then check out with a smile while you're still feeling good, while you still have your mental facilities? Why wait for some new infection to take over your brain, turn you into a vegetable? I'd rather make the decision to die, tell my loved ones that they've helped me have a great life, and then, good-bye."

Unfortunately, the dying are not always able to ensure that their dignity will be respected, so it's up to their loved ones to fight for it: If you know what a loved one would want or what would maintain her dignity, insist upon it.

For Miriam the problem was not her own death, but how she could help ensure a dignified death for her twenty-seven-year-old daughter, Gail. "My daughter is going to die. That's reality. Unfortunately, I'm no stranger to death. When my grandmother was in the hospital, I went to see her a couple of months before she died. She was always the neatest, cleanest woman I ever knew, perfectly groomed, never a hair out of place. I was horrified when I saw her. Her hair was greasy, she could no longer care for herself. Now she could only manage a sponge bath. She was confined to a wheelchair.

"Grandma held my hand and said that she wanted to go. At first I said 'No, Grandma, you've got a long time left, you've got to fight.' But I stopped and listened to what she was telling me. She was saying that she no longer had her dignity, and she wanted to go. I let go of her then, because I knew she was ready to go. It wasn't up to me to tell her when it was time. She had already decided.

"Now my daughter has HIV. At some point, she will decide that she is ready to go. It may be because she can't stand being sick, or the pain, or the feeling that there's no point going on. And the reason won't matter. When she's ready, then it's time.

"I want her to be able to use whatever time she has left to find peace. And I want her to die with dignity. I want her to be surrounded by people who care about her, who aren't afraid of her because of her disease, who aren't ashamed of her. If she can't take care of herself, if she's in diapers or something, I want to be the one to take care of her, if it's okay with her, because I love her. I'll make sure she's treated with dignity. She has that right. I know what I want for her, but I won't let it interfere, with what she wants. I don't care how much longer she has to live. If she has five years, I want her to have five happy years. I can't change what has happened, I can't fix the problem, I can't change the fact that she is going to die, but I can make sure that she has dignity."

FINDING PEACE IN DEATH

Peace is a state of mind. It's a quiet acceptance of what is happening, no matter how chaotic or difficult the situation may be. If you have found a quiet and still place in your mind, you are at peace.

Death is like a storm. It is primitive, it is chaotic, it is a force of nature, and it wreaks havoc on our lives. But like the silence I found in the eye of the storm, it is possible to find peace in the chaos, in the suffering, and in the dark lonely nights. It is possible to find peace in every death. You can only find it by removing everything else. When you release your anger, hatred, and unresolved feelings, there is nothing left but peace. When you are at peace with yourself, you can die in the eye of the storm.

10

NOT DYING ALONE

The right not to die alone.
The right to die in peace and dignity.
The right to be treated as a living human being.

One day in the early 1980s I received a frantic call from the manager of an apartment house. "I knew something was wrong," she said, "I hadn't seen Richard in days. He didn't look good last time I saw him. His car was in the garage so he had to be there. I knocked and knocked. Finally I heard a sound and thought I'd better get my master key and go in." Inside the apartment she found Richard in the bed where he had lain for over four days, unable to get up, unable to even to go the bathroom. He was weak, emaciated, and dehydrated, lying in a wet, soiled bed.

I hurried over to assist, horrified at the site that greeted me. He was so unkempt and dirty I wasn't even able to tell his age. He could have been twenty-five or sixty years old. Seeing this inhumane sight in a modern-day apartment was surreal. I reached for the phone to summon help, but Richard didn't want me to. "No, don't call the paramedics or my doctor or anyone. I am dying and no one can stop that now."

Richard was right, he was dying. "Let me at least clean you up and make you comfortable." I said.

He weakly waved me away with his hand. "I have AIDS. You shouldn't come near me. Just let me die."

AIDS was still largely unknown in the early 1980s. People were afraid of the disease. I was afraid, too, but I could not let someone die like this. "If I protect myself, will you let me help you?" I asked. Richard agreed. I asked Madge, a middle-aged nurse, to help me. We returned garbed in isolation gowns, gloves, and masks, protected not only against AIDS but also from the fallout from a nuclear explosion.

Within a few hours we had this still weak, thirty-four-year-old man cleaned up and sipping soup in bed. Now there was time to talk. "What happened?" I asked.

"It's all there," he answered, pointing to the tape recorder lying next to his bed. "I talked to it. I didn't have anyone else, so I talked to it. You can listen if you want," he said quietly. I left Madge to watch Richard and went into the other room, where I anxiously rewound the tape.

I heard Richard describe how he had been admitted to the hospital, how his doctor told him that he had AIDS. There was no cure, the doctor had said. There's no treatment and he was going to die. His doctor then said he did not want to take care of someone who had "done this to yourself." While he was in the hospital he was left all alone. The food trays were set outside the door to his room, no nurses or doctors came to check on him. "If I am going to die alone," he told his tape recorder. "I would rather be at home." So he called a friend to pick him up. No one at the hospital tried to stop him, no one warned him about what he would be facing.

The friend was shocked to see how ill Richard was when he came to pick him up from the hospital. On the way home, Richard told his friend that he had AIDS. "I thought he was going to pull over and leave me on the side of the road." The friend rolled down the windows when he discovered that his passenger had the dreaded disease. He sped up so as to get Richard home and out of his car as soon as possible. "I got home," Richard continued. "I called another friend, I called my parents. They wanted nothing to do with me. I never felt so alone. I knew then, I would never be hugged or touched again by anyone."

Fortunately, Madge and I were able to convince Richard that he would not have to be alone. He agreed to a new doctor, to fluids and home nursing. Madge went to his apartment every day to feed him, clean him, change his sheets, and give him pain medications. She also gave him something he desperately needed in his condition: companionship. Richard died just one week later with Madge holding his hand.

Perhaps the saddest thing we can think of is being alone when we die. Throughout life we desperately want to connect with others, acquaintances, friends, family members, or loved ones. We become sad when those connections are broken by arguments, divorce, or distance. Losing these connections is even sadder when we face death, when our need to be with others who care for us is greater. That's why *not* dying alone is a fundamental right.

HOW WE ISOLATE THE DYING

Death is by nature one of the most isolating experiences we can ever have. Unless we die in an accident with others, we die alone, the only one dying at the moment. This aloneness is compounded by the fact that we isolate each other at this crucial time.

We isolate the dying by waiting in the waiting room and having our loved ones cared for by strangers.

We isolate the dying by no longer talking to them and no longer listening to them. Sometimes we're not with them physically; more often, we're no longer with them emotionally.

We isolate the dying by no longer talking about what's going on. The widely held notion that the dying do not want to talk about death is a myth. They *do* want to talk about what is happening to them. Aileen Getty described how she ran into Timothy Leary several years ago outside the Viper Room, the club where young actor River Phoenix had died of a drug overdose. Aileen and Timothy hadn't seen each other for some time, so they immediately began catching up. In no time at all they acknowledged that they were both facing terminal illnesses: Aileen had HIV, Timothy had prostate cancer. "We immediately became inseparable," Aileen said. Her choice of the word "inseparable" was profound, for it indicated how separate from the world these two people were feeling. In a certain sense we will all be alone when we die, for death is, by its nature, an act of separation from people, possessions, and the world. No one can die with you, it's a solo activity. Those of us who will survive cannot understand what the dying are going through, physically or emotionally.

"Timothy was so grateful that I asked him about his dying," Aileen told me. "He said he had been waiting for so long to talk honestly about it with someone who would really understand."

When people talk to those who are diagnosed with a terminal illness, they naturally have difficulty understanding what the other is feeling deep down. But Aileen and Timothy were both literally living with the knowledge that they would die, possibly soon. They had a level of awareness that they could share, an awareness that you and I simply could not be a part of. I said to Aileen, "I can imagine that someone over-hearing your conversation about death and dying would think that it sounded offensive or crazy. I can imagine the person overhearing it would want to rush in and say, 'Buck up!' or 'Don't give in,' or 'Don't talk that way!'"

"Yes," she replied, "and that's how they leave us alone. By not being a part of our reality."

We isolate the dying when we refuse to look at the world as they do. But there's no reason why we can't understand that both the living and the dying are in the same boat. The dying may be leaving sooner than the healthy, but it is still the same boat.

Not all communication with the dying need be verbal. Some of the greatest and most profound communication occurs without language. I have been at many bedsides watching two people just looking at each other: one lying in bed the other sitting nearby, not saying a word, but you could tell that their communication was continuing and intense.

Many years ago, a woman told me how hard it was for her to face the imminent death of her son. It was even more diffi-cult because she couldn't share her feelings with her husband. "He won't talk about his feelings," she said. "Sometimes I feel so isolated. So sometimes I go to my neighbor and I sit and cry with her." When I asked her what her neighbor says in reply, she said: "My neighbor doesn't have to say anything, she doesn't have to ask why I'm crying. She lost her son, too. I can just go in and cry. Without either of us saying a word, we know."

We don't always have to have exactly the right words to say to our loved ones who are dying. It's okay just to be with them without saying anything. The point is to be there for them. Our love and understanding will make themselves known.

Not being alone at death means different things to different people. To gray-haired Miriam, a divorced woman who raised her only child by herself, not dying alone means being cared for by people who are not afraid of you because of your illness.

One evening Miriam sobbed as she told me how she responded when her daughter Gail told her that she had HIV. Sitting at her mother's kitchen table one afternoon, the usually bubbly and energetic daughter looked tired and haggard. She told her mother that she had been suffering from a long flulike illness, and had been unable to hold much food down for weeks. After more talk, the daughter tonelessly told her mother that she had contracted HIV. Miriam instantly wanted to hug her daughter, to hold her in her arms as she used to, and make everything better again. But she knew that she could not make things better again, for Gail or for herself. Miriam sat quietly, afraid that she would fall apart emotionally if she said or did anything.

And so the two sat at the small kitchen table, as Gail recited in a detached, clinical way what she knew of the disease, the medicines, the number of years she likely had left to live, and the pain she feared she would suffer. The first bit of emotion crept into her voice when she described how AIDS can sometimes effect the skin, causing purple lesions. "Soon I'll be the ugly lesion queen," the beautiful young woman laughed bitterly.

Unable to hold back any longer, Miriam leaned across the table to her little girl, grown up but still her little baby. But that only made Gail sadder. "Mom," she said, "now that I've got HIV, no one will ever kiss me again. They're too scared."

The brave mother immediately pinched Gail's face together and kissed her. "I'm not scared of you, honey," she said, crying. "I don't know what's going to happen to you, I can't promise it'll all be all right. But I'm never going to pull away from you. If you need a hug or a kiss, I'll give it to you. I gave you your first kiss when you came into this world, and I'll give you your last when you leave this world."

We are afraid of intimacy in our daily lives. Imagine how we run from that kind of closeness as someone we love is dying. But when you hold the hand of a dying person, if you really let yourself be close, you experience some of life's most pure and honest moments. We don't like to get physically close to the dying, and we usually don't touch them. But I have seen nothing more heartwarming than a man holding his wife in his arms as she died. There is no safer place to die than in a loved one's arms.

LOVING HANDS

During another conversation with Aileen Getty, I was struck by her description of death as a "team sport." She pointed out that we're all playing on the same team: We are all born, we all live, and we all die on the team together. The cancer clinics I visited in Tijuana seemed to understand that death is a team sport. They strongly suggested that someone come with you when you checked in, and there was no extra charge for the companion. In fact, they felt that the husband, wife, son, daughter, friend, or whomever you brought along was an integral part of the therapy. But our medical system can be the most isolating in the world. We don't invite our loved ones in, we restrict their visiting hours. Instead of holding them at bay, we should use their love to help us through our last moments.

Dr. Katz shared with me the story of the thirty-five-year-old man, an obese minister, who came into the emergency room one morning terribly short of breath. Panting, the minister explained, that he had to be "fixed up and out" that same day, because he had to do church the next morning. Thinking that he might have pneumonia or possibly a pulmonary embolism, the doctor performed a thorough examination, initiated treatments, and sent the minister to a nearby department for more tests. While being tested, however, the minister suddenly clutched at his chest and collapsed.

"We were working on him for twenty minutes," Dr. Katz said. "His family, who had brought him, and who had no idea this was happening, were downstairs at the coffee machine. When they came back we had to tell them that he was dying. Can you imagine their shock? They said they wanted to be there, they wanted to be with him while we were trying to resuscitate him. This was the first time in my career any one had ever asked for this. I brought them in because I realized this was the last time they were going to be with him, alive. They deserved it. I told the nurses to be as calm as possible, and I told the family members what to expect.

"I've seen lots of people die, I've been through a lot," the doctor continued, "but I never saw anything that made me cry like this. One of his sisters stood by the bed crying, saying, 'Please don't go, please come back.' I've seen people doing this after death, but when you see it happening while someone is still alive, teetering, it's amazingly poignant. The family stayed in there until I pronounced him dead.

"It's amazing we don't do that more often. People should definitely be able to be present when their loved one dies, for their sake. I usually write an order in the patient's chart that says family members can be there twenty-four hours a day, for their sake and for the sake of the person dying."

As Reverend Mark Vierra, a Religious Science minister in Los Angeles, says, "Loving hands greeted us when we entered this world, loving hands will greet us when we leave."

BEING THERE

A deathbed is a very intimate place. We are sometimes not sure whether we should be there, whether our presence would be meaningful or an intrusion. Sometimes the answer may be clear, for we may be the only one there for the dying person. Other times it is not so clear. One day I received a call from Gary. Upset, he told me that his friend from junior high school was dying of a malignant glioma, a type of brain tumor. Gary had already visited him once in Hawaii, and didn't know if he should be with him. He had asked his friend's wife and parents if he should be there, but they did not give him an answer. They were not sure what he should do. I told him to stop looking for permission from other people, to decide if it was right for him to be at his friend's deathbed.

I wasn't suggesting that he intrude where he was not welcomed, but on the other hand, he shouldn't look to others to tell him what to do. I reminded him that the wife and parents were wrapped up in grief. And like the rest of us, they were undoubtedly unprepared for the death of their loved one. How could they have answers for him?

Whether you should be at someone's bedside is a personal matter that only you can settle. The key questions to consider when making your decision are: Have you said everything you needed to say? Do you feel moved to be there? What if he died tomorrow and you weren't there?

Sometimes, despite our best intentions, our loved ones die alone. They may want it that way. Grace, whose son Jeff was dying, had regrets about not having been there for him in the past. She was determined to be there now. Toward the end, Grace became fixated on being at the bedside at the moment Jeff died. He was glad she was there, but often needed more space than Grace gave. He frequently asked her for private time.

One day she announced: "I was there when you came into the world, I will be there when you leave."

He replied, "Mother, it's only important that you are here now. My death will happen the way it's supposed to happen. I don't want to leave you with any regrets. Maybe I'll want to die alone. It may feel like a private thing to do. Maybe I'll just think it will hurt you too much. I won't know either until I get there. It's the love that's ultimately important, not where we are at a certain time."

Grace heard his words, but was still determined to be there. She didn't leave the house at all during the last few weeks of his life, even though there were nurses and other loved ones present around the clock. As Jeff inched closer to death, she barely left the bedside. The night he died, she stepped away briefly to go to the bathroom. It was in these couple of minutes that he passed away. Grace had to come to terms with the fact that death has a life of its own, and comes when it wants to, not when we want it to.

Sometimes we're supposed to be there, and sometimes we're not. If you and your loved one feel that you would like to spend this most precious moment together you can certainly try, but remember that fate has a way of stepping in to make its own decisions.

Companionship

Project Angel Food is a nonprofit organization in Los Angeles that delivers meals to men, women, and children with AIDS. I was a member of the board of directors, and later became the organization's president. Marianne Williamson, the project's founder, instilled a philosophy that remains alive: "We are not just delivering meals to people with life challenging illness. We are also delivering companionship." For many of the people we served, knowing that someone was coming to visit that day was as important as the hot meal they received. Many volunteers pushed through their fears to be there for someone else.

People also push through their fears by being with friends and loved ones. Lawrence, the thirty-seven-year-old with Hodgkin's disease, has been in remission for eleven years, but he has seen death and thought about his own. The process has made him more comfortable with the end of life, and taught him the importance of not letting anyone die alone.

"Our instincts are to pull away when someone is sick or dying. I've been close to a couple of people who were dying and I feel it makes a positive difference in the quality of their lives. I've noticed with people who are dying that the worst thing is to be alone. It's inhumane to be alone. It's better to have people with you laughing and smiling or crying and commiserating until the end. We are screwed up about dying in our culture, we don't know how to do it. My first time was with my dad, in 1985.

"Dad had lung cancer. It freaked me out. Even though I saw him six hours before he died, I didn't feel that I was there with him through the process. We didn't speak about death. He only hedged by saying I should take care of Mom if something happened to him. There was no frankness, no real communication. I was there for him physically, but not emotionally, which means that we both missed something important.

"When he died, I refused to go see the body. I was scared, I didn't want to see him dead. I had just seen him before he died and wanted to live in that moment. I really didn't realize that was my last chance to see him. Now I'm sort of ashamed that I wasn't there. Even though it would have been difficult, I could have been present."

It was not surprising that Lawrence was not able to be there as much as he would have liked to for his father. None of us are comfortable while watching our loved ones die. However, once we have gone through the process with a loved one, we feel more comfortable being there than not being there.

As he went through the deaths of several friends, Lawrence learned how "to let death onto my landscape. It's like a wake-up call telling you to go visit them if they're sick, be there for them.

"I was only there at the moment of death once, for Bill, someone I knew through AA (Alcoholics Anonymous). His cancer started in the lung, then metastasized into his bones. I was the last person to be with him. That was three years ago. He withdrew a little bit toward the end, then his friends began to visit him. I hadn't seen him in a while so I called and he said to come the next day. It was his final day. He was mostly unconscious, no longer communicating well, but he recognized me. I felt special that he asked me to come over. He hadn't showered in a long time, he didn't look good, yet he said, 'Yes, come over.' I felt honored.

"Bill's death was the most peaceful I've seen. He chose where he wanted to die, at a friend's house, in a comfortable bed. He took time in the last few weeks to visit with people. He didn't pursue things medically, he decided it was time for him to go. He made his decisions about death and kept control of his dying. He created a quiet exit. He remained himself. His friends stayed themselves. He was the same in his last two weeks as he was normally. He had dignity. He died in character. He was fifty-six when he died, the same age as my dad. I grew a lot with Bill's death."

With each death we learn how to do it a little better, we become more experienced and comfortable with an experience that is never in itself comforting. We learn that the only thing that can sometimes comfort us, or our loved ones, is our presence. There are no instructions; it's a process of trial and error, learning as you go. We all have the right not to die alone. It's much better for the dying and for the living if we do it together.

II

THE BODY

The right to expect that the sanctity of the body will be respected after death.

Death has become increasingly impersonalized in the past 100 years. In days past, the ailing were cared for by their families. When they died, their bodies were cleaned and dressed by those same families. Friends came to console the families in their homes, and the deceased were often laid to rest in the family plots. There was a connection to those bodies and to the people in those bodies, a connection that went from birth to death and after. Now we die in hospitals, sometimes in hospices, but rarely at home. Strangers pick up our loved ones' bodies and cart them off. We don't see them again until the funerals, if at all. We wonder and worry: Where are you going with my father's body? How do I know that you're going to care for it properly? How do we know that our religious traditions will be honored?

Besides fearing that our loved ones' bodies won't be treated with dignity, we're confused about so much concerning our dying and death rituals. We may want to be with our loved ones when they die and in the moments thereafter, but are unsure if we're allowed to do so. We wonder if we can have a party to celebrate the lives of the deceased or if we must mourn their deaths with a traditional funeral. We may want to personally scatter a loved one's ashes in a favorite place or put them on the mantel in a beautiful vase. Most of all, we want to say good-bye in our own loving, respectful ways, but we aren't always prepared to do so because we have so little experience with death that we don't really know our options. Most of us are guided though a funeral home by counselors we've never met before, making choices through veils of shock and grief.

From the moment our loved one breathes his last breath to the final hugs and handshakes with our friends and family at the funeral service, we feel confused, rushed, frightened, and grief-stricken. As a result, we often walk away from a funeral service, our final ritual, feeling empty. We look back on our loved one's death wishing that somehow it could have been different.

THE MOMENT AFTER DEATH

One summer evening, Sara, the seventy-year-old retired college professor who insisted to her doctor that she had a right to hope, began hospice care. Sara was hoping for a quick death, for her abdomen was filled with tumors and her time was drawing near. Hugh, her husband, said, "I want Sara's death to be a more peaceful situation than when we brought my mother home to die ten years ago. Time seemed to slow down as Mother approached death. It became surreal. The seconds became minutes, the hours became days. Then all of a sudden, in the midst of this slowness, she died. Suddenly everything sped up tremendously. We were in a state of shock. We thought we were prepared, and yet it was different than anything we could have imagined. Time just accelerated, and I mean really accelerated, and we and our grieving were left behind.

"It began by the doctor calling, the relatives coming over, the nurse was there, Uncle Henry was on the phone wanting to know what happened, the mortuary guys showed up to take Mom away. The paramedics came, I don't know why. The undertaker wanted to discuss the arrangements. We had to call relatives in England right away because they wanted to come to the funeral. This all happened within ten minutes of her death, all while I'm trying to get a few minutes alone with my mother. Things are going crazy and the next thing I know she is being carried out on a gurney. I never got to say good-bye to her."

"I don't want that to happen when I go," Sara said gently.

I reassured Hugh and Sara that we would do everything we could to keep things as peaceful as possible. Two nights later the kind woman died at twenty past midnight. Hugh and their eldest son had been there for many hours, hanging on to her every breath. The moment she died, the nurse called her doctor, letting him know what had happened. In California, if the cause of death is known and the deceased has been seen by a physician within the last sixty days, the doctor will usually sign the death certificate. That way the death is not a coroner's case, and thus the paramedics and police are not involved. The doctor was asked if the nurse on duty might pronounce Sara dead, and if he would sign the death certificate. He agreed. Once he said yes, it was okay for a medical professional to remove Sara's tubes.

I explained the situation to Hugh and his son, what the nurse was doing and why, adding: "I know you wanted to call your other two children when it happened. How much time do you need for them to come over?"

After his two calls to the children, I called the mortuary, telling them that the family wanted them to wait two hours before Sara's body was removed. Many people don't realize that you can ask the mortuary to wait a reasonable amount of time—up to two or three hours—before coming to pick up your loved ones. This allows family members time to be notified and to say their final good-byes. For some, these last moments together are very important, much more so than any moments at the funeral or memorial service. These moments give loved ones time to adjust to what has happened, and to spend some private time with the deceased. Many people feel that this frees them up to be consoled at the memorial.

With the mortuary notified to wait two hours before arriving, I told Hugh and his son that the nurse and I were "going to straighten up while you're calling people to let them know. We'll come and get you in a few moments." While they were out of the room making their calls, the nurse disconnected Sara's IVs and other machines, moving as much medical equipment away from the bed as possible. She changed the sheets, covered her with a fresh top sheet, and I closed her eyes with my fingers. In other cases, I've seen the nurse wash the deceased's face or brush the individual's hair. The dying often have a high fever before death, and may have been restless or too pain-sensitive to be properly groomed. Often, if there are flowers around and it's appropriate, I put them on the nightstand or the bed.

I called Hugh back into the room to spend time with Sara. When I'm present at the moment of death, or shortly after, I try to make sure that everyone has some time alone with the deceased, often encouraging them to touch or speak to their loved one, if they want. Many people don't know that they are "allowed" to do this. They're often afraid to ask, but are very grateful if given "permission." The final moments together, alone, give people a clear sense that their loved one is now gone.

Hugh and Sara called each other "Bunny" because, early in their relationship, they gave each other little pecks on the lips which they called "bunny" kisses. Friends heard them referring to each other as "Bunny" and began calling Hugh and Sara "the Bunnies." It was like a second last name for them. They gave each other bunny calendars and key chains, little rabbit figures, and other items. Soon friends began doing the same, and during the many years they spent together they developed the largest collection of bunny items you can imagine. Now Hugh spent some time alone with his wife for the last time, telling her that he was glad she was no longer in pain, no longer sick, and that she was at peace. "We've raised wonderful kids, Bunny. Don't worry about them or me, we're going to be just fine. How could we not be, having had such a wonderful wife and mother? When it's my time to die," he said, "I hope you will be there, waiting for me with bunny kisses."

The son who was present said his private good-bye to his mother, as did the other two children when they arrived. Then they all gathered as a family, one last time, with their mother, each touching her and comforting one another with tear-filled eyes.

When the mortuary people arrived, I suggested to Hugh, his children, and relatives that they wait in a distant room while Sara's body was removed. I assured Hugh that I would watch over her remains. In other cases, loved ones have preferred to be there every moment. Many people feel that watching the body leave is very disturbing. The warm memories are replaced by colder ones of a body bag being wheeled out.

The most important thing to remember at this difficult moment is that *you can take time* to spend a few quiet moments with the deceased. Unless there is reason for this to be a coroner's case, you can take some time to assemble your family and grieve.

Once the person has been removed, many families and nurses like to make the bed, tidy up the room, perhaps put flowers on the bed. They do this because people tend to gravitate toward the bed, wanting to see the last place their loved one was.

How We Say Good-bye

Rituals are an important part of our lives. They mark transitions, they are rites of passage. We have many deeply meaningful rituals—weddings, bar mitzvahs, confirmations, and last rites. Perhaps the most important of these is the funeral ritual. The funeral, the final telling of the deceased's story, helps us to accept the reality of death. It may also help us through the process of mourning. An example is one found at Jewish funerals: all the loved ones and friends, one by one, take a shovel with dirt and throw it on the casket. It is a final completion and helps mourners accept that the person has died. It is also considered to be the final act of love, since this kindness cannot be repaid.

There are many elements to our funeral rituals, including removal of the body from the place of death, washing of the remains, embalming, viewing of the body, a funeral service, a headstone or other memorial. These may or may not be important to us. Before Kevin, the artist, died, his friends asked him what he would like for a memorial. He characteristically said: "I don't care. I'll be dead. It's up to my friends to decide if they want anything." When Kevin died they decided that they wanted to hold a memorial service for him. "We did it for us," one friend said. "Formally saying good-bye to our friend, together, was an important part of our grieving process."

In different cultures and times, a death was mourned by friends, family, and even the person who expected to die soon. This approach was described in a document called *"Ars Bene Moriendi"* ("The Art of Dying"), prepared in Europe in 1348, during the bubonic plague. People planned their own memorials before they died, rehearsing their funerals just as we rehearse our weddings. In that plague-ridden time, they believed that dying would be easier if they were more comfortable with their own deaths.

Some people prefer to emphasize the feeling of loss, looking for a way to share their loss collectively. They often turn to passages from the Bible or to poems that express the deep sorrow they have trouble expressing individually. Others prefer not to emphasize the sadness and grief. Instead, they want to think of their loved ones as, in a sense, living on forever.

During the past several years, I have seen more and more people trying creative, unique ways to emphasize their loved ones' lives rather than their deaths. In some cases, sad memorial services have been replaced by gatherings celebrating the deceased's life. Sometimes it works, sometimes it does not. I have been to very festive, celebration-of-life gatherings, with balloons and pictures of the deceased, their favorite music playing, people taking turns telling funny stories about the loved one. We left those celebrations with a real sense of who the deceased were, grateful to have known them, feeling almost as if they had given us a piece of their joy as a going-away present. I have also been to a celebration where it seemed as if someone was missing, and we wondered why we were doing this instead of holding a memorial service. For some people, a party or celebration would be sacrilegious or appalling and disrespectful. Others feel that it's the greatest honor you can give the deceased. It's up to you to decide if it's right for you.

Celebration-of-life parties are not the only new idea. Pensacola, Florida, is home to "Junior's Funeral Home," which features perhaps the nation's only drive-up viewing window designed for the convenience of those who have difficulty getting out of their cars and into the chapel. This is a unique way to view an open casket, yet those who use it feel quite serious about paying their last respects to their friends.

Sometimes, unfortunately, our grief is lost in the multitude of details one can get caught up in while planning a funeral. It's not unusual for people to get so caught up in planning the funeral that they don't take the time to grieve. Sometimes grief is deliberately shoved aside, or taken advantage of. An example of this occurred when Rudolph Valentino died unexpectedly while in New York for the premiere of his latest movie, *Son of the Sheik*. The studio that had made millions on the career of this young actor, only in his thirties, orchestrated a mob scene when his body was removed from the hospital where he had died of peritonitis. The studio arranged for his body to be viewed in New York then transferred via rail to Los Angeles, where another mob scene had been arranged. All this was done to glorify his image and promote his movie. Things were progressing well, as far as the studio was concerned, until, at the last minute, they realized that no one had arranged for a final resting place. A friend saved the day by giving up her space in her family plot for Valentino.

The actual funeral ritual, whether it is a traditional funeral, a cremation, a Dixieland jazz funeral, or maybe even a drive-through mortuary, is not as important as the spirit with which it is carried out. Most people want something that reflects the way the deceased lived and respects the way they want to be treated and remembered.

A FINAL RESTING PLACE

How we treat the remains of our loved ones is a reflection of our feelings for them and their lives. We reinforce the concept that their life meant something by going to great lengths to give a proper ending to their life, especially if it's a tragic ending. We honor their lives with a "proper" burial or cremation. We do it for them, and for us, for it gives us a sense of finality and completion. Many family members and friends of victims whose bodies were destroyed in tragedies have described how hard it is to grieve and find some sense of closure without the body. Putting them to rest is good for us, the survivors, for it helps us to find closure. It is one of our noblest acts of love for the deceased.

We respect the body of our loved one by placing it to rest in a place they have designated or we believe that they would appreciate. Some choose to be buried in a family cemetery; others choose cremation, which is becoming more popular. Many feel that cremation is a practical and inexpensive option to traditional burial, and the loved one can be kept in a special place at home. Many people prefer to be buried for religious reasons, and/or so that their loved ones will have a place to visit them.

Many choose to be scattered at sea or another favorite place. Louise Hay put her mother's ashes under a small budding tree in her backyard. When we spoke, Louise showed me how much the tree has grown, and how she enjoys seeing it reaching toward the sky. Then there are some very nontraditional ways of handling a loved one's remains. Timothy Leary's ashes were scattered in outer space. One woman I know was not sure what to do with her mother's ashes. She consulted a friend, who told her to put them in her mother's favorite place. So the woman carefully placed her mother's ashes in her handbag, drove into Beverly Hills, and spent the afternoon at her mother's favorite upscale department store, scattering her mother's remains in the plants! I tell this story to illustrate how unique people can be, although I do not recommend that you break any laws.

Some are less concerned about their final resting places, choosing instead to help society, or try to return to it, by donating their bodies to medical science or having them cryogenically frozen, hoping to be defrosted and restored to life at some point in the future.

Sometimes, when there are no remains to be buried, or your loved one is buried far away, the survivors feel empty. They want someplace to go, someplace that represents or reminds them of the deceased. Many cemeteries offer a solution to this problem: a cenotaph, a very small plot of land where you can place a plaque or headstone and "visit" your loved one. Sometimes we don't know where a person will be buried but would like to honor them. That's why it's now common for people to put flowers where a person has been shot or killed in a car accident. It's a way of offering respect to the deceased, commemorating their life by commemorating their death. The Vietnam Memorial in Washington,

D.C., serves a similar purpose for the loved ones of those who perished without remains to be buried or properly revered.

Regardless of the place and style of the final interment, we should do what is meaningful for us and for the departed.

HOW WE REMEMBER

When I was just a little boy, my cousin Sylvia taught me that the greatest gift we can give our loved ones, the way we can honor and respect them the most, is by remembering them. For example, Jewish people remember their loved ones who have passed away by lighting a twenty-four-hour candle on the anniversary of their death. In the Catholic Church, a mass may be offered in memory of the deceased.

We also remember in less formal ways. Skinny was the large, rotund owner of a bar called Skinny's. When Skinny died, all his pals, including his best friend, Rodney, spent the day at Skinny's drinking toasts to their good friend and recounting the many funny and nice things he had done. At first Rodney's wife was appalled by this. She thought it was disrespectful of the men to be drinking in a bar when their friend was not even buried. But one of the wife's friends explained to her that what the men were doing made perfect sense: They were honoring their friend by sitting where they had sat with him so many times, by drinking the beer they had shared with him, and by sharing their recollections of the man. "It's the same as if one of our friends died," she said. "We're Italian. We cook. We'd get together in the kitchen and cook and talk about her. You remember someone by doing what you always did with them, even though they're gone."

Remembering our loved ones' does not have to be a morbid experience. Ed's Coffee Shop is a popular lunch spot in Los Angeles. Ed and his wife managed Ed's for thirty-seven years. Then Ed passed away and his wife retired, so their daughter now runs the small coffee shop. She's covered the walls with poster-sized pictures of Ed. If I said to you, "Let's go have lunch at a coffee shop with pictures of a dead person hanging on the walls," you would think it grim and morbid. But as far as the customers are concerned, the place is filled with warm memories and wonderful photos of Ed. One customer who has been coming since the day it opened, shared with me, "It just wouldn't be Ed's without Ed. We wanted the photos up."

Sometimes we don't have to do anything specific to remember our loved ones. Instead, we show our love and respect by continuing on in place of our loved ones, by remembering who they were and what they stood for. I recently attended the wedding of Shawn, whose older brother, Ron, and I had been good friends. As I stood watching the beautiful bride walk down the aisle, I remembered Ron, her beloved brother. I wondered if he could see his sister's wedding through my eyes. His sister, the bride, felt that Ron was represented by myself and his other friends.

I had a similar experience when I attended the citizenship ceremony for Janine. She and her friend Steve had come to Los Angeles from their native Australia some time ago. The two "Aussies" remained best friends until Steve died an early death. I knew how much this moment meant to Janine, and what it would have meant to Steve. As I watched Janine take the oath of allegiance to the United States, I felt that Steve was with us that day. Many people feel that the deceased can really see through our eyes and attend events with us after their death.

Rituals

Many people wonder what they should do when a loved one dies. The best you can to is to be true to yourself and your deceased loved one. During these times most people find comfort in the rituals of Christianity and Judaism, as well as other belief systems.

Your heart will rarely lead you astray. If your heart tells you to follow the burial and mourning rules of the loved one's religion, then do so. Everyone deserves a memorial that honors his or her beliefs. The more you deviate from the norm, the more resistance you'll encounter from others, but follow your heart and be true to your loved one. I remembered how much my father had liked the blue blazer and pink shirt that he bought for what turned out to be his last birthday party. When the funeral counselor told me to bring a suit with a white shirt for my father to be buried in, I said that the blue blazer and pink shirt would be better. This upset the counselor, who insisted that a white shirt was preferred. I replied, "My father is not a white-shirt person. This last outfit, which he loved, is the one I'm choosing."

When performing the rituals surrounding death and funerals, it's very easy to get caught up in doing it the "right way." There is no right way; there is only your way or the way your loved one wanted to be treated. However, rituals give us structure, and they help many.

Accept your own feelings. People sometimes tell me, quietly and with much guilt, shame, or puzzlement, that they feel glad, almost happy that their loved one has passed on. I point out that this is nothing to be ashamed of. We forget how much we suffer with the dying. It's natural to feel relief when we realize that they are no longer in pain, they can no longer be hurt, they are no longer diseased, they are no longer sick or suffering—that a major burden has been lifted from them and us. The pain, the burden, the disease is what we're happy is gone, not our loved one. It's also perfectly legitimate to feel happy that you have your life back. You gave freely of yourself when you were needed. Now you are glad to return to your own life, as your loved one would have wanted.

Talk about the dead with each other after the funeral. Use this time to mourn and grieve with others who share your love, your sadness, and your memories. The love and togetherness shared in honor of our loved ones are a wonderful posthumous gift to them.

Treat the things your loved one leaves behind just as you would were they still alive. The day after Sara died, I stopped by her house. Hugh and his two sons were sitting among friends while his daughter was in the bedroom packing her mother's personal items and undergarments. She later told me she took such care because: "It's my way of respecting her. Mother was very private about her body in life, so I feel she should receive the same respect in death. I know she would want me to pack up her private things and take care of them quietly."

If you are in a situation where others are more grief-stricken than you, there are many ways to help. Share a funny story about the deceased, or bring some food to their house. If you see that the dishes need washing or the flowers need watering, simply take care of it for them. Don't ask how you can help. Look around to see what needs to be done and do it. If there's nothing to do and you have no touching stories to share, just be there.

Death is difficult to accept, but it's even harder to deal with when it strikes suddenly, unexpectedly. There is no warning, no notice, no chance to say good-bye.

One recent morning there was a message on Sharon's

answering machine from Florence's son, Jackie. Florence had been like a second mother to Sharon, whose real mother had died when Sharon was young. Florence guided Sharon through childhood, and she was there for Sharon in her teenage years. Once, when Florence took Sharon to the Music Circus in Sacramento, she said to the young girl: "I'll take you to the Circus until you're old enough to take me." Florence gave Sharon the sense of family she lacked. Twenty years passed and Sharon was well into her thirties but Florence, Jackie, and Sharon were still like family. Then Sharon got that phone call. The message simply said, "Please call me right away. It's an emergency." Time stopped when she heard those words, for she knew something was seriously wrong. Sharon called back Jackie within the hour, who told her that Florence had died of a massive heart attack.

Sharon was in shock, she couldn't believe that Florence was dead. She had just seen her two weeks ago, there was still a message from the older woman on Sharon's phone machine from the night before. How was it possible that she was gone? When Jackie asked Sharon if she wanted to fly up to Sacramento early to view the body, Sharon replied: "No, I'll be there for the funeral." A few minutes later she called back to say that she did want to see Florence's body. She felt that she had to, otherwise she couldn't believe that her friend and surrogate mother was dead.

A few hours later, Sharon was standing by the lifeless body in the funeral home. Florence looked asleep, her body untouched by the ravages of old age or disease. "She was lying so peacefully I almost believed that if I shook her shoulder and whispered her name, she would wake up and we would go to the Music Circus together."

"In my private time with her," Sharon said, "I said good-bye. I thanked her for her kindness and love. I was grateful for this opportunity to be with Florence. I felt I was given an intimate opportunity to grieve that I probably would not have had at the memorial service. Had I not seen her, I might have postponed grieving by letting myself pretend to believe that she was not dead, that she was just "away" somewhere. This was the dose of reality I needed." If you don't have this opportunity, you can find other private ways to say good-bye. You can spend time with something that reminds you of the person, maybe a special place you shared. Or just sit alone, quietly letting memories of that person fill your heart.

A BETTER DEATH

I hope that you and your loved ones will have a gentle experience of death. I believe that by helping others die in a way that honors them, we teach each other and our next generation how to die and perhaps make our own deaths more meaningful. I believe the more comfortable we become with dying, the more fully we can live. I believe that though we may not always like its appearance, we should treat death as naturally as we treat birth.

On my last visit with Elisabeth Kübler-Ross, we spoke about the ending of her first book, which I have always felt contained a beautiful analogy: "Those who have the strength and the love to sit with a dying patient in the silence that goes beyond words will know that this moment is neither frightening or painful, but a peaceful cessation of the functioning of the body. Watching a peaceful death of a human being reminds us of a falling star: One of a million lights in a vast sky that flares up for a brief moment, only to disappear into the endless night forever."

The dark night sky we call death holds the essence of courage, compassion, sacredness, and authenticity. I wrote this book hoping that you can find tenderness, kindness, and love on this final journey you or your loved one may now be taking. I believe there is no better way to honor ourselves, our lives, and our loved ones, than by honoring the rights of the dying.

My own earliest and most significant encounter with death—my mother's—occurred when I was twelve years old. Mom had battled illness throughout my life. For years she had been in and out of hospitals, always recovering, always hopeful. Finally, she lay in a hospital in New Orleans, gravely ill. My father and I sat outside the intensive care unit for days, in shock, only being allowed to see her for ten minutes out of every two hours. And not just any ten minutes of the two hours; it was exactly 10 A.M. to 10:10, then 12 noon to 12:10, and so on. In fact, they were so strict that when my cousin Sylvia flew in from Boston and rushed to the hospital, the "timekeeper" nurse refused to admit her, for she had missed the visiting time by two minutes, and would have to wait two hours. The nurses restricted the visiting hours so harshly for the physical benefit of the patients. It was simply easier for them to care for the patients without the family always there. This infuriated cousin Sylvia, who was also a nurse. When Sylvia left New Orleans she drew the "time-keeper" nurse aside and to talk to her about the incident.

The nurse said, "You don't understand, visitors get in the way of my work."

Sylvia said: "You're a disgrace to your profession."

The nurse haughtily replied: "I have a job to do."

"I'm her family," snapped Sylvia. "I have a job to do too."

Luckily, there were many other nurses who were caring and compassionate and who went beyond the call of duty. It was, nevertheless, a harsh environment. Mom was in a ward with seventeen other patients, with only curtains for privacy. But the nurses didn't like the curtains closed, for then they could no longer see the patients. You had to be fourteen to visit the patients and I was only twelve, so I constantly feared that the nurses would deny me access to my mother. Many of the nurses didn't enforce the age rule, but a few were extremely strict. My mother was dying and I relied on complete strangers to grant me the right to see her.

After eight days of waiting and hoping, my father and I were told there was no chance she would recover this time. The doctors said that we should "let her go." We reluctantly agreed. Before the next visiting period came, the doctor told us that she had passed away. My father asked if we could see her. The doctor very reluctantly agreed to let my father see her, but said that I could not, for I was too young. But when the nurse came to lead my father to Mother I went along, hoping to not be caught.

The nurse led us to Mother's bed, where her body now lay lifeless. I remember thinking how much more at peace she looked without all the tubes and machines attached to her. I also remember how removed from her I had felt during those last visits, with a respirator going, an oxygen mask covering her face, three to four IV lines, the dialysis hookup. Imagine how hard it would be for anyone, much less a child, to complete or find closure or any kind of intimacy in this stark, institutional setting. I was relieved to at least be face-to-face with my mother without all the machines and tubes. Still, I felt little privacy, for the other seventeen patients in the ward were there. And the nurse stood right by us at my mother's body, never leaving us alone, prepared to whisk us out when our brief, allotted time was up.

My eyes were drawn to Mother's hand, which I could see under the sheet. I wanted to hold her hand, I wanted to caress it. I wanted to talk to her, out loud, to tell her that I loved her and to say good-bye. Instead, I stood with my arms at my side, silent, feeling I did not have permission to move or speak in this sterile environment.

Perhaps because of the closeness I was denied, the lack of intimacy and inability to complete my relationship with my mother, I later insisted that my father and I fly immediately to Boston, where she was to be buried. I wanted to go right away so that my mother's body would not be alone for even a minute in Boston while waiting to be buried. My father agreed and we flew to Boston that night. There, I learned that Mother's body was not going to be sent from New Orleans for a few days. Mother's body was alone during that time. And I felt all alone.

Fortunately, things have improved in hospitals since this occurred twenty-four years ago. Finally realizing that family and friends can be a great "medicine" for patients, hospitals have expanded visiting hours and otherwise made it easy for people to visit. Hospitals now treat the deceased with much more respect than they used to. In Dr. Mark Katz's busy emergency room, when someone dies the family is given time to come in to see their loved one. That's not easy to do, given the space and personnel restrictions, especially in an emergency room, where the emphasis is on the living. But Dr. Katz and others like him feel that it is the right thing to do.

When my father was facing death in the late 1980s I was grown up, changed both outside and in. I was determined to have a better experience of death with my father than I had with my mother. I brought my dad into my home, making sure that he was surrounded by loved ones and cared for at all times. When he died, I made arrangements with the mortuary for me to come early to his memorial, to spend time alone with him, to sit with him, just the two of us, in a private room. I didn't plan what I would say or do, for I knew that I would be swept away by my feelings, that it would come very naturally.

My father and I used to sing together, so I sang to him again in the same heartfelt way you might sing to a sleeping baby. All alone in the funeral home, standing by his coffin, I sang "Let Me Call You Sweetheart," the song he used to sing to my mother.

While I always thought of it as a romantic song between lovers, in that moment it didn't seem to be a love that was restricted to husbands and wives. "Let me call you sweetheart. I'm in love with you. Let me hear you whisper that you love me, too. Keep the love light glowing in yours eyes so true. Let me call you sweetheart, I'm in love with you." It felt like a song about tenderness, and having a sweet loving heart. Now when I hear the song unexpectedly, I think of them, I think of love, and I think of the kindness and love we all deserve, especially at the end.

Epilogue

A MESSAGE FOR THE DYING

As you read this you may be beginning your last months, days, or hours here on earth. You have traveled on a long and winding road on this journey that we call life. Many philosophies teach that what you feel and experience in the last moments of this life are the seeds of your next one, of your new life.

None of us know what will happen from here, but if you look deep inside, deep in your soul, you will know that birth is not a beginning and death will not be an ending. If you think back, you'll remember that you never felt as if you didn't exist before you were born into this life. Rather, you felt as if you have always existed and always will. That's why this death will not be an ending. You may not have life as you know it once you die, but you will continue. You will take all of our love and all of your memories with you on your journey. What you have experienced will not be lost, neither will your life be lost. Whatever you may feel about your life, whatever has happened, *has happened*. And that was your life. Try to accept that it was your life, just as it was. No better and no worse.

As this life draws to a close, it is time to let go of your anger, as well as your love. You have worked; you have worried; you have driven hard; you have loved and laughed; you have been angry and disappointed. It is now time to rest, time to relax. There is nothing else for you to do. There is no other way for you to be. If you find yourself becoming frightened, rest and relax into your breath. Your breath will take you where you need to go. Know that those around you who may cry and scream are doing so because they do not know how to say good-bye; they are doing the best they can. And know, in your heart, that you will leave part of yourself behind with everything you have done, with everyone you have ever met, with every life that you have touched. You will also take a part of us with you.

If you still feel attached to the right and wrong of your life, know that right and wrong are now over. You experienced life exactly as you were supposed to. You were born for a reason, and you will die for a reason. You were born whole and innocent, beautiful and worthy, and you will die that way. You have spent time and followed time; now time will be no more. You will go to a place where we already are. You were carried off in the miracle of birth, and so you will be carried off in the miracle of death. All that we are, all that we have felt for you, all the love that was given to you, will be your cushion on this journey. Now you will begin. I wish you love, peace, and a safe passage. It is now time for you to return home.

A MESSAGE FOR THE LIVING

I understand how hard it is for you to watch someone you love slipping away. The pain is excruciating, the feeling of devastation unmatched by anything you have ever known. Losing a loved one is one of the hardest experiences any of us will have to face, but there are some things that you can do to make it easier on yourself and those around you:

Allow yourself to grieve. You can't ignore it or run away from it: Eventually it will catch up with you. Grief is a necessary part of the healing process. It will subside, but you must go through the various stages.

Don't feel guilty because you are continuing to live. You are not responsible for what has happened. Accept that some things are out of your hands.

Let the dying know that it's okay to leave—that you'll be all right without them. You'll miss them for the rest of your life, but you would not want them to stay if it continues their suffering.

Don't feel guilty if you find yourself preparing for your loved one's death. This is a natural occurrence—it's not an insult, and it won't hasten the death. But it does help prepare you for the inevitable and is nature's defense against deep pain. (The ancient Egyptians spent their entire lives preparing for death.)

Say what you want to say now, while there's still time. You may still have something to say or something to do for your loved one. "Do it fearlessly," one patient told me. Let your loved one die with an open heart—yours.

To the best of your ability, try to accept what is happening and the way it is happening. As difficult as it may be to understand and accept, dying is a part of life.

Take care of yourself and let others support you. Seek help from a therapist, a support group, your religion, or whatever else comforts and strengthens you. Try to stick to some kind of regular routine, especially during this very stressful and upsetting period. Believe it or not, it will help normalize your life and make you feel better.

Above all, be gentle with yourself. It really will get better with time, although you may not believe it right now. Time heals all wounds, and although your loved one will no longer be physically present, you will always retain the love you have shared with that person. Those whom we've loved and who have loved us in return will always live on in our hearts and our minds.

I wish you peace and healing.

Acknowledgments

This book did not begin when I finally sat down to write it. It began years before when I was given the privilege of caring for wonderful patients who became my friends and teachers. First and foremost, my heartfelt thanks goes to them.

I am also deeply indebted to the colleagues who have shown me so much support over the years, including Marianne Williamson, whose years of love and friendship have been matched only by all that I have learned from her work, and Elisabeth Kübler-Ross, M.D., for her advice, guidance, wisdom, and friendship. Thanks to Mark Katz, M.D., for letting me spend time in his emergency room, and for his medical review of this book. Thanks to James Thommes, M.D., for his medical review, for letting me call him daily with questions, and for being a great friend through all my adventures. Thanks to Elizabeth Taylor for her leadership, compassion, and unwavering commitment in the fight for care and dignity of people with HIV. And grateful appreciation to Mother Teresa for the simple kindness she showed me. The Missionaries of Charity are truly an inspiration and gift to the world.

Thanks to my agent, Al Lowman, at Authors and Artists

for his early encouragement and confidence in my work. He helped mold an idea into a book that seeks to restore power to our loved ones in their final chapter of their life. Thanks to Mitchell Ivers at HarperCollins, whose honesty, insight, and editing talents were truly a gift for a first-time writer. And thanks to Barry Fox for helping me with structure and making me explain everything.

Thanks to Linda Hewitt for her confidence in me, for always being by my side, and for being so dedicated to the quality of every project. And thanks to my dear friends, family, and colleagues: Robert Alexander, Howard Bragman, Janine Burke, Elaine Chaisson, Ph.D., Gary Chin, Pharm.D., Nastaran Dibai, Aileen Getty, John Gile, Jacob Glass, Jackie Guzman, Susan Habif, M.S.W., Mary-John Hart, M.A., Jeffrey Hodes, Katrina Dibai Hodes, Sylvia Hunt, R.N., Wayne Hutchison, R.N., Judith King, Joni Marshall, Ann Massie, Robert Matt, Jerry Milliken, Cathy Parks, Berry Berenson Perkins, Ed Rada, Teri Ritter, R.N., Pam Saffire, Trent St. Louis, Reverend Sandy Scott, Jaye Taylor, Richard Taylor, Steve Tyler, Steve Uribe, M.F.C.C., Reverend Mark Vierra, and Chantal Westerman. The love, support, and contributions offered by these wonderful people made this book possible.

My love and thanks to those who now live in our memories: Barbara Caplan, Steve Draine, Randy Frizzell, Harriet Ivers, David Wm. Johnson, Ron McGuire, Steve Oldfield, Louis Paskin, Anthony Perkins, Tom Proctor, Ron Rose, Dan Stone, Sam Williamson, and Florence Zissimatos.

Thanks to Arnold Fox, M.D., Rabbi Ben Zion Bergman, Father Leo Hoar, and Reverend Ronald David Beams and Keith Green for their time and openness.

Finally, thanks to my goddaughter Emma Williamson, who is teaching me about life from the beginning.

A Note on Sources

I am deeply grateful to the workshop members of the Southwestern Michigan Inservice Education Council whose work over thirty years ago created "The Dying Person's Bill of Rights," which was the inspiration for this book.

On page 65–66, the mnemonic **"ABCDE"** comes from: Jacox A, Carr DB, Payne R, et al. *Management of Cancer Pain*. Clinical Practice Guideline No. 9 AHCPR Publication No. 94–0592. Rockville, Md. Agency for Health Care Policy and Research, U.S. Department of Health and Human Services, March 1994.

The information on page 66 about patients taking strong medications and rarely exhibiting addictive behavior comes from: Portenoy RK, Payne R. "Acute and Chronic Pain." In: Lowinson JH, et al, eds: *Substance Abuse: A Comprehensive Textbook*. 2d ed. Baltimore: Williams & Wilkins; 1992, pp. 691–721.

The suggestion on page 72 for round-the-clock pain control is in Jacox, A., op. cit., p. 45.

The mention of Dr. Dyer's approach to spirituality on page 98 comes from his book entitled *Your Sacred Self*. New York: HarperCollins, 1992.

The letter-writing technique presented on page 101 is explained in *A Return to Love* by Marianne Williamson. New York: HarperCollins, 1992, p. 209.

The reference on page 126 to Kathleen McCue comes from the book she wrote with Ron Bonn titled: *How to Help Children Through a Parent's Serious Illness: Supportive Practical Advice from a Leading Child Life Specialist.* New York: St. Martin's, 1994.

The concept of the angel of death on page 137 is from: Marianne Williamson, *Illuminata*. New York: Random House, 1994, p. 117.

The story of Elvin and Sara on page 155 is from: Boxall, B.: "Families' Tales of Anguish, Suffering," *Los Angeles Times,* March 7, 1996, p. A16.

The story of Harold's mother on page 158 was described in: Boxall, B.: op. cit.